A TEXTBOOK OF AGRICULTURAL EXTENSION MANAGEMENT

A TEXTBOOK OF AGRICULTURAL EXTENSION MANAGEMENT

C. Karthikeyan
R. Sendilkumar
D. Jaganathan

ATLANTIC
PUBLISHERS & DISTRIBUTORS (P) LTD

Published by

ATLANTIC

PUBLISHERS & DISTRIBUTORS (P) LTD

7/22, Ansari Road, Darya Ganj, New Delhi-110002
Phones : +91-11-40775252, 40775214, 23273880, 23275880
Fax : +91-11-23285873
Web : www.atlanticbooks.com
E-mail : orders@atlanticbooks.com

Branch Office: Chennai
Phones : +91-44-48531784, 28291383
E-mail : chennai@atlanticbooks.com

Printed & bound in India by Atlantic Print Services

Foreword

Utilisation of resources has been the most common and yet perhaps the most complex human activity ever since the dawn of civilisation. Management is the process of utilisation of resources in an effective manner in today's dynamic environment. Management is a catalyst without which no organisation can survive and grow. Today the art and science of management and its application has become crucial for the success of any organisation. The scientific knowledge is indispensable for a deep understanding of the nature, importance, functions and other aspects of management.

It is well known that management is recognized as a profession and it is a systematic and specialised body of knowledge consisting of principles, techniques and laws and can be taught as a separate discipline or subject. This is a comprehensive book on Management in which the important aspects have been explained clearly. An effort has been made by scientists to compile information and to present them in most easy and understandable manner for the benefit of students of various disciplines like Management, Agriculture, Dairy Science, Home Science, Rural Development, Environment, Health, Social Welfare, Extension Education, etc., and it would be of immense help to extension officers, managers, scientists and administrators of various sectors to acquire managerial and technical skills. The entire book is prepared in most simple, clear and talking language so that the contents could be easily followed by the readers.

I am happy that the authors have taken steps to present all the relevant facts related to management in this book. I appreciate their work and I am sure that this book will be very much useful to those who are interested in Management.

C. Ramasamy
Vice-Chancellor
Tamil Nadu Agricultural University
Coimbatore
Tamil Nadu

Preface

Management is the brain of an organization and it is the process of utilization of resources in an effective and efficient manner in the today's dynamic environment. Management today unifies and focuses on the approaches to manage the work of the organizations.

Systematically designed in seventeen chapters, this is a comprehensive and yet self-contained book on Management.

Beginning with the nature, scope, principles and concept of management, it covers all important dimensions of management. Its second chapter provides management issues in organization. The next seven chapters are devoted to planning, decision making, organizing, departmentation, delegation, coordination, budgeting and auditing, focussing mainly on their meaning, nature, principles, different types and importance in management. Human resource planning, demand forecast, supply forecast, human resource information system and human resource audit have been discussed in the tenth chapter. The eleventh chapter provides motivation methods and techniques in which importance of motivation in management is presented. Management techniques like management information system and tools of network analysis are presented in the twelfth and thirteenth chapters, respectively. Management by Objectives, a Systematic Approach and Innovative Approaches are studied in depth in the fourteenth and fifteenth chapters, respectively. The sixteenth chapter discusses management training and development techniques. The final chapter deals with the different management tools like SWOT analysis, Johari Window, participatory rural appraisal, Agro ecosystem analysis, transactional analysis etc., in detail.

For an overall development of the organization, effective management is most essential. With this view, this book has been prepared for educating and motivating the people in an organization. This shall serve as a textbook for students of various disciplines like Management,

Agriculture, Dairy Science, Home Science, Rural Development, Environment, Health, Family Planning, etc., and it would be of immense help to extension officers, managers, scientists and administrators of various sectors to acquire managerial and technical skills.

The authors express their grateful thanks to the several sources from which they have drawn information for writing this book and welcome any suggestions for its improvement.

C. Karthikeyan
R. Sendilkumar
D. Jaganathan

Contents

1

The Concept, Nature and Principles of Management

Introduction

Management is guiding human and physical resources into dynamic organizational units which attain their objectives to the satisfaction of those served and with a high degree of moral sense of attainment on the part of those rendering service. Utilization of resources has been the most common and yet perhaps the most complex human activity ever since the dawn of civilization. Management came from the French word and its meaning is 'house keeping'. Management is the process of utilization of resources in an effective and efficient manner in today's dynamic environment. Management is not restricted to factory, shop or office. It is necessary for business firms, agricultural firms, Government enterprises, educational and health services and so on. The emergence of giant corporations in large numbers has necessitated the growth of management as a discipline. It has drawn knowledge, tools and techniques from a number of disciplines and that is why it is known as interdisciplinary.

Definition

Management is the art of getting things done through other people.

—Parker Follet

Management is defined as the process by which a cooperative group direct action towards common goals.

—Joseph Massie

Management is the process of planning, organizing, leading and controlling the efforts of organizational members and of using all other organizational resources to achieve the stated organizational goals.

—*Michel H. Mescom*

Agricultural Extension Management may be defined as the process of planning, organizing, leading and controlling to accomplish organizational objectives in the field of agricultural extension through the coordinated use of human and material resources.

Nature of Management

(i) Management is a process.
(ii) It is purposeful.
(iii) It is a human activity.
(iv) It is a integrative force.
(v) It is a social process.
(vi) It is universal.
(vii) It is needed at all levels of the organization.
(viii) It is dynamic.
(ix) It is a group phenomenon.
(x) It is getting the things done.
(xi) It is intangible.
(xii) It is both a science and an art.
(xiii) It is a profession.

Scope of Management

(a) Subject matter of management

Subject matter includes the entire process of management *viz.*, planning, organizing, staffing, directing and controlling.

(b) Functional areas of management

1. Production management: It deals with plant site, plant layout, work measurement, production planning and control, etc.

2. Financial management: It includes financial planning, management of earnings, capital, capitalization, capital structure, management accounting, budgeting control, cost control, etc.

3. Personnel management: Deals with manpower planning, job analysis, recruitment, selection, orientation, placement, training and development, compensation, promotion transfer, social security and labour welfare, retirement, industrial relations, etc.

4. Materials management: Includes inventory control, material control, purchasing, materials handling, transportation, etc.

5. Marketing management: Includes the marketing process, marketing planning, marketing mix, market segmentation, marketing information, marketing research, etc.

(c) Management is an interdisciplinary approach

For the effective application of management principles, theories and techniques, a study of commerce, economics, psychology, sociology, mathematics, etc. is also required.

(d) Universality of management principles

The principles of management have universal application.

Differences between Administration and Management

Sl. No.	Administration	Management
1.	Formulation of broad objectives, plans and policies	Art of getting things done through other people
2.	Decision making function	Executive function
3.	Decides what is to be done and when it is to be done	Decides who should do it and how it should be done
4.	Thinking function as far as planning and decision making is concerned	Doing function and managers get the work done under their supervision
5.	More important at higher level of management	Important at supervisory or lower level of management
6.	The term administration is used more frequently in non-business organizations like Government offices, military organizations, etc.	The term management is used more frequently in the case of business enterprises.
7.	Administrators are generally owners of business enterprises	Managers are generally employees of the enterprises, who are paid remuneration

EVOLUTION OF MANAGEMENT THOUGHT

Schools of Management Thought

1. Management by custom schools: This school considered empirical experiences to be of great value from which generalizations can be deduced.

2. Human relations school: This school laid emphasis on the human component and other allied aspects like leadership, communication and motivation. Concept of getting things done with and through people.

3. Sociological school: This school envisaged an organization as a segment of the society rather than hierarchical system. This school further emphasized upon the need for understanding organization relationships, group reactions and the influence of informal organizations—so vital for the organizing function of management.

4. Decision theory school: This school viewed management as essentially a process of decision-making.

5. Mathematical or Quantitative measurement school: This school thought that managerial problems could be converted into mathematical models which could be deployed for the solution of managerial problems. This school further brought into play the use of tools and the techniques like linear programming, simulation, queuing theory, gaming theory, decision tree and the like as analytical aids to decision making.

6. Management process school: This school of thought believed that management was a process consisting of basic functions for getting things done through other people.

7. Contingency approach: This approach to management emphasizes the fact that management is highly practice oriented and action packed discipline managerial decisions and action initiatives are to be matters of pragmatism and not of principles. The environment of organizations and managers is very complex, uncertain, ever changing and diverse. The choice of approaches as also their effectiveness is contingent on the behaviour and dynamics of situation variables. Management theory and principles tend to be deterministic or dogmatic approaches.

Contribution of F.W. Taylor (Scientific Management)

Frederick Winslow Taylor was the first person who gave the scientific management. He is also called as the father of scientific management. Taylor started his career as an apprentice and turner in cramp shipyard in Philadelphia, U.S.A. After three years he joined in Midvale Steel works.

After two years he was promoted in Gang Boss. After four years he was promoted as chief engineer. After that he left this organization in 1898 and joined Bethelehem Steel Company where he remained till 1901. After that he became a consultant and devoted his life for the cause of management.

Definition

Scientific management means knowing exactly what you want men to do and seeing that they do it in the best and the cheapest way.

Philosophy of Scientific Management.

Science, not a rule of thumb.

Harmony, not discord.

Cooperation not individualism.

Maximum output, in place of restricted output.

Development of each man to his greatest efficiency and prosperity.

Contribution of Henry Fayol (Modern Management)

Father of modern management is the French industrialist Henry Fayol (1841-1925). Trained as a mining engineer, he made his mark as an industrialist with the French coal and iron combine of Fourchambault, where he spent his entire working career. He joined the firm as a junior executive in 1860 and rose quickly through the ranks, retiring as a director of a company in 1918. Fayol had the opinion that his success was not due to his personal abilities as a manager but due to the methods he used. He felt that management was not a personal talent but a skill. He published many books and papers on management. However, the most important was his book entitled *Administration Industrielle it Generate* written in French and published in 1916 which contains his principles of management. He divided the total activities of an industrial undertaking into the following six groups:

1. Technical (Production)
2. Commercial (Buying, selling and exchange)
3. Financial (Search for and optimum use of capital)
4. Security (Protection of property and person)
5. Accounting
6. Managerial (Planning, organizing, commanding, coordinating and controlling).

Taylor Vs Fayol Contribution

Taylor gave importance to the need for systematic management, to analyse the work to be done, to measure it and to assign portions of work to the people best selected and trained to perform that work. His main contribution was not in the area of general or top management. It was essentially around shop floor or plant management. His main ideas are given below:

Separation of planning from doing.

Manager to plan in advance the work to be done.

Manager to select and train the workers on scientific ideas.

Manager to rearrange to conduct time and motion studies.

Differential wage plan.

Functional foremanship and division of labour.

Standardization of tools, equipment, working conditions, etc.

Fayol on the contrary gave the principles of management. He divided the managerial activities into six categories viz., technical, commercial, financial, security, accounting and managerial activities. He also Explained the functions of management. However, his main contributions to the evolution of the pattern of modern management lies in his:

Giving us overall concepts of general management.

Introducing with great emphasis the principles of unity of command and unity of direction.

Pointing out the importance of non financial incentives.

Emphasizing the planning functions of top management.

Identifying the key problem of delegation and decentralization of authority.

Both are responsible for the managerial revolution that has taken place during the last seven decades. The main difference between the two is that while Taylor worked primarily on the operative level from the bottom of the organization hierarchy upwards, Fayol concentrated on the managing director and marked downwards on the organization hierarchy. Taylorism has undergone a profound change under the impact of new developments. Fayol's principles have withstood the test of time and have been accepted as the core of management science even at the present time.

PRINCIPLES OF MANAGEMENT

Henry Fayol stated that the principles of management are not rigid. On the contrary they must be capable of adoption to various enterprises and settings. He has given the following principles:

1. Division of work: Division of work means specialization. Job and work should be divided into small elements and each element should be assigned to the specialist of that element. It promotes efficiency because it requires an organizational member/group to work in a limited area and thus enabling the member/group concerned to develop specialization due to repeated exercise in that limited area.

2. Authority and responsibility: Authority and responsibility should go together. The right and power to give orders should be balanced with the responsibility for performing necessary functions.

3. Discipline: Discipline in terms of obedience, application, energy and respect to superiors requires good superiors at all levels.

4. Unity of command: A subordinate should receive orders from only one boss. If the unity of command is violated, 'authority is undermined, discipline is in danger, order disturbed and stability threatened'.

5. Unity of direction: Each group of activities having the same objective must have one head and one plan. It will create dedication to the purpose and loyalty.

6. Subordination of individual interest to general interest: The interest of the business enterprise ought to come before the interest of the individual worker.

7. Remuneration: Remuneration should be fair and adequate. It should afford the maximum satisfaction and include both types of incentives, financial and non-financial.

8. Centralization: There should be one central point in the organization, which exercises overall direction and central of all the parts. But the degree of centralization of authority should vary according to the needs of the situation.

9. Scalar chain: The line of authority from the chief executive at the top to the first line supervisor at the bottom must be clearly defined.

10. Order: This applies to both materials and men. An organization ought to be based on an orderly and rationally thought out plan.

11. Equity: Management in dealing should exercise kindness and justice with its subordinates. This will create loyalty and devotion among the employees.

12. Stability: It is linked with long tenure of personnel in the organization. Efficiency is promoted by a stable work force.

13. Initiative: The ability to think afresh and in advance would act as a powerful motivator of human behaviour. Plans should be well formulated before they are executed.

14. Esprit de corps: Union is strength. The, whole organization should work as a team and every team member should work for accomplishing goals.

Functions of Management

Management is the brain of an enterprise without which no organization can survive and grow. The following points highlight the importance of Management:

- It is the management, which makes the people realize the objectives of the group, and directs their efforts towards the achievement of these objectives.
- Management is a way to utilize the resources optimally. Through better planning, sound organization and effective control, management enables a concern to reduce costs and enable an enterprise to face competition.
- Management ensures efficient and smooth running of business.
- Management provides new ideas, imagination and visions to the organization.
- Management moulds the enterprise in changing environment.

Goals of Management

The goals of Management can be summarized as below:

- To achieve increased production, reduced costs and maximum efficiency.
- To provide trained and efficient work force.
- To standardize methods of work, materials and equipments.
- To develop science for each element of a man's work.
- To replace old thumb rule.
- To select, train, teach and appoint workmen scientifically.
- To promote cooperation.
- To ensure division of work and responsibility.

Bureaucracy in Management

Characteristics of bureaucracy include:

Specialization and division of labour.

Hierarchical positions.

A system of abstract rules.

Impersonal relationships.

Employment is based on technical qualifications.

The bureaucrats are protected against arbitrary dismissal and promotions are made according to seniority/ achievements.

Manager

Manager is a person who has the art of getting things done through other people:

He has formal authority (*i.e.* Right to command).

He may or may not have personal power.

Manager is appointed and after that gets a position in an organization.

Management as a Profession

Edgar H. Schein has compared key qualities of professionals with those of managers. In particular, he notes the following three characteristics:

Professionals base their decisions as general principles.

Professionals achieve professional status through performance.

Professionals must be governed by strict code of ethics that protects their clients.

McFarland has pointed out the following characteristics of management as a profession:

Existence of an organized and systematic knowledge.

Formalised methods of acquiring training and experience.

Existence of an association with profession with professionalisation as its goal.

The formation of ethical codes for guidance and conduct.

Charging of fees for service rendered.

Kennith Andrews identified the following characteristics of management as a profession:

Knowledge

Competent application

Self control

Social responsibility

Community sanction

LEVELS OF MANAGEMENT

In an organization there exists a chain of superior— subordinate relationship. Various managers are linked with one another through the vertical chain. Levels of management suggest the arranged managerial positions in an organization.

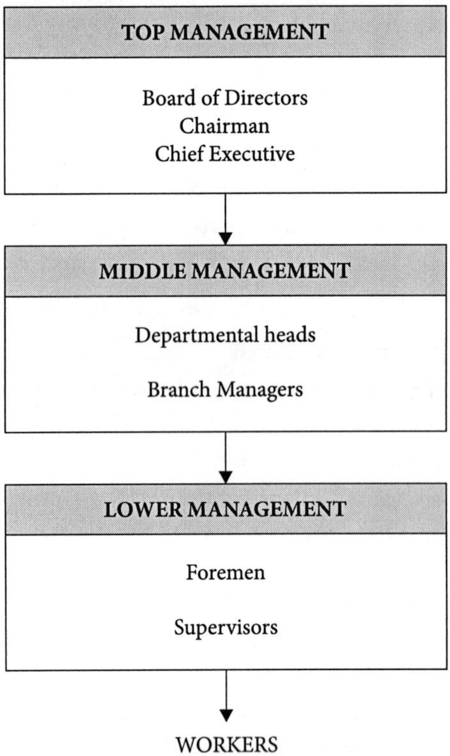

Fig. 1. Levels of Management

The levels of management determines the authority and status of managers. There is no fixed number of management levels. However, the different levels may be classified into three categories as shown in Figure 1.

1. Top management
2. Middle or intermediate management
3. Lower or operating management

Top Management

Top management of a company consists of Board of Directors, Chairman, Chief Executive, etc. Top management is the ultimate source of management authority and it is accountable for overall management to the shareholders of the company. The main functions of top management are as follows:

- Determining the objectives of the enterprise as a whole.
- Setting up of an organizational framework.
- Framing policies and making plans to achieve the objectives laid.
- Work as a link between internal organizational environment and external environment by representing organization.
- Assembling the resources of men, machine, material and money.
- Providing overall leadership to organization.
- Exercising effective overall control.

Middle Management

Middle management consists of departmental heads which are generally classified under upper middle management and deputy heads of departments and sectional heads, area managers, etc. It is basically concerned with the task of implementing the policies and plans laid down by the top management. The important functions of middle management are as follows:

- Interpreting the policies framed by top management.
- Selecting suitable operative and supervising personnel.
- Assigning duties and responsibilities for timely execution of the plans.
- Motivating personnel to achieve higher productivity.
- Preparing the organizational set up in their respective departments.
- Compiling and issuing instructions to the supervisors under their control.
- Coordinating with other departments so as to ensure a smooth running of the entire organization.
- Reporting feedback to top management.
- Collecting information and reports on performances.
- Making recommendations to top management for the better implementation of plans and policies.

Lower Management

Lower management or operating management or supervisory management is the lowest level of management. It includes plant superintendent, front line supervisors, sales officers, etc. They are concerned with day-to-day planning and implement the policies of middle management. They pass on the instructions of middle management to the operatives and translate the plans. The various functions of lower management are as follows :

To issue orders and instructions to the workers and supervise and control their functioning.

To plan 'the activities of his section, classifying and assigning jobs to the workers.

To direct and guide the workers about work procedures. To provide on the job training.

To solve the problems of the subordinates.

To communicate the problems upward in the hierarchy which cannot be solved at this level.

To maintain discipline among the subordinates, and develop in them the right approach for work.

To build up a high group morale among the subordinates.

To maintain good human relations.

To act as a liaison officer between the middle management and rank and file employees.

Skills in Management

Different types of skills are required to manage effectively a large organization. These skills can be classified as:

1. Conceptual skill
2. Human skill
3. Technical skill

1. Conceptual skill: It is the ability to integrate and coordinate the various activities. A manager needs to have the qualities or skills so as to be able to view situations and coordinate various factors.

2. Human skill: A manager has to get the things done through other people and hence he must have human skills or ability to select, motivate, guide, lead, direct and control people.

3. Technical skill: A manager must have the necessary technical skill or ability to work with the resources, tools, techniques, procedures, etc. The degree of technical skill required varies with the level of management.

Fig. 2 shows that the conceptual skill is required most by top-level managers. Middle-level managers require conceptual and technical skill equally because they are the bridge between top managers and lower management people. As the work of lower management is operative, they require technical skill the most. Human skill is required by all the managers as they are with the people and have to deal with people at all levels.

Roles of Manager

Roles are organized set of behaviours. These are behavioural patterns. Henry Mintzberg classified the manager's roles into three areas, interpersonal, informational and decisional. Managers have formal authority, status, personal characteristics and skills to perform these roles effectively (Fig. 3).

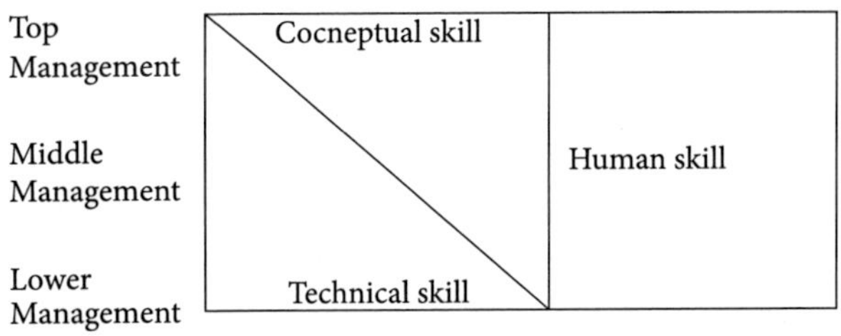

Fig. 2. Managerial Skills at Various Levels

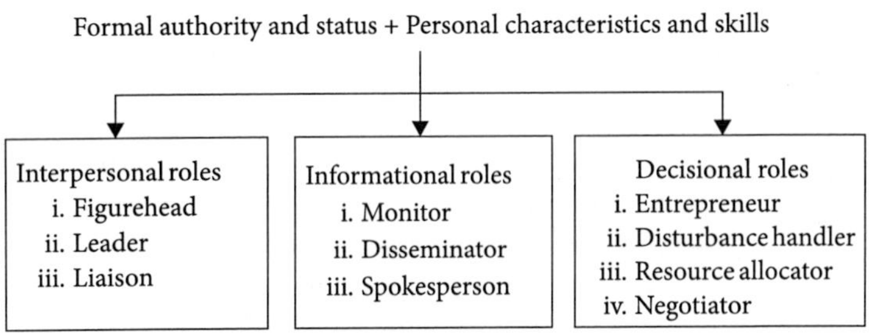

Fig. 3. Roles of Manager

1. Interpersonal roles: There are three interpersonal roles inherent in the managers' job. This set of roles derives directly from the managers' formal position. As the figurehead for his unit, he stands as a symbol of legal authority, performing certain ceremonial duties, e.g. signing documents and receiving visitors. The manager in a leader role hires, trains and motivates his personnel. In the liaison role, manager interacts with many people outside the immediate chain of command, those who are neither subordinates nor superiors.

2. Informational roles: They are important because information is the lifeblood of an organization and the manager is a receiver and collector of information. Information is acquired through meetings, conversations or documentation. In the disseminator role, managers disseminate information to subordinates daily. As a spokesperson the manager transmits information to individuals outside the organization.

3. Decisional roles: To get the work done, managers have to make decisions. Managers act as entrepreneur, disturbance handler, resource allocator and negotiator. In playing the entrepreneurial role, managers actively design and initiate changes within the organization. As a disturbance handler, the manager handles difficult problems and non-routine situations such as strikes, energy shortages, etc. As resource allocator, the manager decides how resources are distributed. With respect to negotiator role manager negotiates with suppliers, customers, unions, individual employees, the government and other groups.

Styles of Manager

(i) Autocratic wants to run the show all by him

(ii) Laissez faire or free rein managers permits his followers to do whatever they want to do

(iii) Democratic style is based on the assumption that the manager derives his power by consent of the followers. Participation, consultation and agreement of the group members are important features of democratic style.

Strategy building

Strategy refers to the interpretative plan proposed in the light of prevailing circumstances and likely future events in order to secure a position advantageous to the enterprise.

In a broad sense a strategy means preparing the organization for unforeseen and unpredictable situations e.g. price control by the Government, strike call by the trade union, price cutting by competitors, etc. Thus a strategy is a plan prepared to employ the forces of the organization most effectively in order to accomplish the desired goal.

A strategy is a gamesmanship or administrative course of action designed to achieve success in the face of the difficulties. It is the ground design or the overall plan, which a company chooses in order to move or reach the objectives. It seeks to provide the optimum match between the firm and its environment.

Strategy building procedure

The process of strategy formulation has the following steps:

Determination of objectives

Ascertaining the specific areas of strengths and weaknesses in the total environment

Preparing the action plan to achieve the objectives in the light of environmental forces.

Types of strategies

(i) **Master strategy:** Also called strategy implies the entire pattern of goals, policies and resource deployment of an organization. It provides unified direction to the entire organization.

(ii) **Derivative/Programme strategy:** It refers to departmental strategy. It refers to the specific deployment of resources. It is designed to support the master strategy for the achievement of organizational goals.

(iii) **Minor strategy:** Also called as sub strategy and is more specific and detailed. It is prepared to execute a derivative strategy.

FOR DISCUSSION

1. Define management.
2. Explain the nature and scope of management.
3. Differentiate between administration and management.
4. Discuss different schools of thought in management with suitable example.
5. Explain the contribution of father of scientific management.
6. Who is the father of modern management and explain his contribution to management?
7. Discuss the principles of management as given by father of modern management.
8. Explain the functions and goals of management.
9. What is bureaucracy?
10. Define manager. Discuss the roles of manager.
11. Discuss different levels of management.
12. Discuss the types of skills needed by the managers in management.
13. What are different styles of manager?

2

Development Organizations—Role of Public/Private and Other Agencies in Management

The organization involved in agricultural extension management is considered and it can be categorized mainly into two: public funded extension systems (Governmental organizations) and private organizations (Non-Governmental/ voluntary organizations).

Public Funded Organizations

About 85% of extension services around the world are public extension programmes funded by the Governments. The National Extension Service of India is the biggest extension organization in the world. There are many streams of organizations devoted for agricultural extension under public extension systems:

1. ICAR Extension System
2. Extension Systems of the Ministry of Rural Development/State Development Departments
3. Extension Systems of Commodity Development Boards under the Ministry of Commerce
4. Nationalized Banks
5. Corporate Bodies
6. Input Organizations

The ICAR extension system comprises of mainly research institutes and the agricultural universities; the scientists and the extension personnel of these institutions are required to play "First line" extension role through organizing demonstrations, training, etc., on a limited scale, but forceful enough to have catalytic influence on other extension system/sub-systems.

The main agency for agricultural development work is the Ministry of Agriculture and the State Departments of Agriculture. The introduction of Training and Visit System by the ministries was intended to strengthen the extension system considerably for rapid transfer of technology. The monthly zonal workshops held under the Training and Visit System serves as a good mechanism for fostering linkages between research stations and development departments, such as agriculture, horticulture, fisheries, forestry, animal husbandry and agricultural engineering. In the zonal workshops messages are formulated to be adopted the for next month.

The work of commodity development boards of Ministry of commerce is generally limited to a single commodity, such as coffee, tea, spices, rubber, etc. These semi-autonomous public sector firms (Coffee Board, Rubber Board, Spices Board etc.,) provide research, extension, input supply, credit and marketing services for farmers.

Nationalized Banks like State Bank of India, Indian Bank, Canara Bank, etc. have their specific villages/areas of extension servicing for agricultural sector. For technical guidance in crop production, livestock production, fisheries, dairying, etc., they seek the assistance of research stations and colleges of agricultural universities.

Corporate bodies like Neyveli Lignite Corporation, United India Insurance, etc., also undertake limited extension service by organizing training programmes in vegetable cultivation, mushroom production, sapling planting, etc. They also organize environment awareness campaign in their respective townships.

Input organizations like FACT, SPIC and MFL also adopt villages and they organize agricultural seminars mostly in collaboration with KVKs.

Private Organizations (NGOs)

The voluntary organizations and other autonomous/non-government bodies have also been contributing to the rural development work including agricultural extension work.

There is a scheme of income tax concessions under which such organizations are exempted from tax according to the amount spent on rural/agricultural development activities. This has provided a great incentive to the private sector for investment in rural/agricultural development.

There are now quite a few voluntary agencies in the country which have the requisite technical/managerial resources available with them to undertake development projects and to manage them successfully. Bharatiya Agro Industrial Foundation (BAIF) of Maharashtra, MYRADA of Bangalore, Mitraniketan of Thiruvananthapuram, UPASI of Coonoor, etc., are few examples. At the national level, the People's Action Development for India (PADI) seeks to promote voluntary action to supplement governmental efforts in the field of rural development.

Krishi Vigyan Kendras (KVK)

KVKs are transfer of technology project of ICAR and are hosted by ICAR institutes, agricultural universities and voluntary organizations. KVKs conduct need based vocational trainings in agriculture and allied fields to practising farmes, farm women, rural youths, tribals, etc., under the integrated model of KVK, the erstwhile, lab to land programme, National Demonstration, SC/ST projects.

The Indian extension system has to manage 81.5 million land holdings and about 750 million farmers, farm women, young farmers and agricultural labourers. Any extension system/ sub-system, however, vast cannot reach them quickly. Therefore, in Indian context multiplicity of extension agencies, training institutions, input organizations, etc. and duplication of work by them is a misnomer. What is required is to develop and maintain strong functional relationship and play complimentary and supplementary roles influencing the total agricultural production in the country.

MANAGEMENT ISSUES AND THEIR IMPLICATIONS

A. Some of the controversial issues in organizations

(i) ***Art and Science:*** Whether management is a science or an art is an ongoing debate/issue among management scholars. Some experts contend that management is really an art, something that can only be learnt by experience.

Some other people are of the opinion that management is more a science than an art. Management has a systematic body of knowledge constituting a core of principles and theories that tend to be true in most managerial situations.

(ii) ***Universal concept:*** Some experts do not agree about the universal nature of management. They say management is not universally applicable due to the cross-cultural differences.

Some other experts say that the principles and procedures are applicable universally.

(iii) ***As a profession:*** Hodge & Johnson have defined profession as a vacation requiring some significant body of knowledge that is applied with high degree of consistency in the service of some relevant segment of society. Some say that management is a profession and some others argue that management is not at all a profession.

(iv) ***As a social responsibility:*** Some management experts say that management has social responsibility and some others disagree.

B. There are some other issues in organization, which should be avoided to make organizations more effective

(i) ***Failure to clarify relationships:*** This is the chief source of friction, politics and inefficiency amongst members of an organization.

(ii) ***Failure to delegate authority:*** This creates the need for referring even the trifling problems to the upper levels, overburdening the top executive with details and slowing down decision making at the operational levels.

(iii) ***Delegating authority without responsibility:*** This may lead to organizational anarchy. The subordinate should be responsible to the superior for proper use of the delegated authority.

(iv) ***Multiple subordination:*** The practice of subordinates having more than one person to report may lead to break down in the unity of command.

(v) ***Short circuiting:*** Establishing relationship between superior and subordinate, bypassing one or more levels of administrative hierarchy for communication and action may lead to low morale and lack of initiative amongst the functionaries who have been ignored.

(vi) ***Giving extra constitutional authority:*** Delegating authority by a superior to some selected subordinates of personal choice who are not entitled to it under the rules, may help to develop an autocratic atmosphere and vitiate the working climate of the organization.

(vii) ***Formation of clique:*** Developing narrow exclusive circle by a superior with some selected subordinates may damage the organization to the extent that it may not be able to reach its goals.

Management Properties of Agricultural Extension

Agriculture and rural development programmes are mostly implemented by organizations, which may be Government departments, educational institutes, voluntary organizations or elected bodies like panchayats, etc. They generally try to attain their objectives by improving the rural enterprises through involving research and other support systems on the one hand and the client system on the other. Irrespective of the nature of organization, there are some fundamental principles and methods, which guide their effective functioning. This is called Management:

(i) Management is basically concerned with ideas, things and people.

(ii) Management is concerned with resources, tasks and goals.

(iii) Management is the development of people and direction of things.

(iv) Management is not an inborn but an acquired ability.

(v) Management is any leadership responsibility not just business and industry.

(vi) Flow of information from the research stations to the farmers and of farm problems back to the research stations.

(vii) Production of teaching materials and teaching aids for use in extension work.

(viii) A capable and trained extension staff who can transmit the useful information to the farmers and assist them to organize farming as a business.

(ix) In order to facilitate this movement of information back and forth, the number of levels of extension administration should be kept as small as possible.

Implications

(i) It developed, strengthened and organized the groups, institutions and people to achieve their objectives.

(ii) It developed leadership in local and professional situations.

(iii) It acquainted the planners, policy makers and administrators with local conditions and the latest technologies suited to it.

(iv) It provided sufficient data for developing plans and for coordination of activities.

(v) It gave direction and a package of educational practices for adoption and diffusion and also provides a communication media mix for innovations and evaluations.

(vi) It improved rural people life through their individual and cooperative effort.

Attributes of an Extension Organization

According to Van den Ban (1986) the attributes of an extension organization include:

(i) ***The transfer of knowledge*** from research to the clients who are generally farmers, farm women and rural youth.

(ii) ***Advising clients*** on the decisions they have to make, sometimes by recommending a certain decision to be taken, sometimes by helping them to acquire sufficient insight into the consequences of the alternatives from among which they can choose in order that they can make their own decision.

(iii) ***Educating,*** helping clients to make a decision in such a way that they are able to make similar decisions themselves in the future.

(iv) ***Enabling clients to find their own way*** by helping them to clarify their goals and the possibilities, which they have together with others, to realize these goals.

(v) ***Stimulating*** desirable and sustained economic development.

FOR DISCUSSION

1. Role of different agencies in development.
2. Management issues in an organization.
3. Attributes of extension organization.
4. Implications of extension organization.

3

Administration System Approach to the Planning Process

Planning is the basic managerial function. It helps in determining the course of action to be followed for achieving various organizational objectives. It is a decision in advance what to do, when to do, how to do and who will do a particular task. Planning is a process, which involves thinking before doing.

Definition

The determination in advance line of action by which certain results are to be achieved. Planning is deciding in advance a course of action for reaching organizational goals. The line of action is decided in advance so that actual execution becomes easy later on. —*Hart*

Planning means the determination of what is to be done, how and where it is to be done, who is to do it and how results are to be evaluated. —*James L. Lundy*

Planning is the conscious process of selecting and developing the best course of action to accomplish an objective. It is the basis from which future management decisions spring. —*M.C. Niles*

Planning is an intellectual process that includes the skills of anticipating, influencing and controlling the nature and direction of change. Planning bridges the gap from where we are to where we want to go. —*Me Farland.*

Steps in the Planning Process

Planning process: It involves the setting up of business objectives and allocation of resources for achieving them. Planning determines the future course of action for utilizing various resources in a best possible way.

Following steps are taken in planning process:

1. The first step is awareness of business opportunity and the need for taking action. Present and future opportunities must be found so that planning may be undertaken for them. The trend of economic situation should also be visualized, for e.g., if thinking of the government is to develop rural areas into industrial centers. A beginning should be made early after going through a detailed analysis of the new opportunity.
2. Before actual planning is initiated relevant facts and figures are collected. All informations relating to operations of the business should be collected in detail.
3. Objectives are the goals, which the management tries to achieve. The objectives are the end products and all energies are diverted to achieve these goals. Planning starts with the determination of objectives. The tie between planning and objectives help employees to understand their duties. It is essential that objectives should be properly formulated and communicated to all members of the organization.
4. Planning is always for uncertain future, though may be certain in the coming period but still certain assumptions will have to be made for formulating plans. Forecasts are essential for planning even if all may not prove correct. The success or failure of planning will depend upon the forecasts for various factors. If the forecasts are accurate then planning will also be reliable.
5. The next step will be choosing the best course of action. There are a number of ways of doing a thing. The planner should study all the alternatives and then a final selection should be made. All the pros and cons of methods should be weighed before a final selection.
6. Evaluation will involve the study of performance of various actions. Various factors will be weighed against each other. A course of action may be suitable but it may involve huge investment and the other may involve fewer amounts but it may not be very profitable. So, evaluation is essential for proper planning.
7. Once the main plan is formulated, a number of supportive plans are required. In fact, secondary plans are meant for the implementation of principal plan.

8. The last step in planning process is the implementation part. The planning should be put into action so that business objectives may be achieved. The implementation will require, establishment of policies, procedures, standards and budgets.

Recognizing need for action
↓
Gathering necessary information
↓
Laying down objectives
↓
Determining planning premises
↓
Examining alternative courses of action
↓
Evaluation of action plans
↓
Determining secondary plans
↓
Implementation of plans

TYPES OF PLANS

1. Operational, Tactical and Strategic Plan
2. Proactive and Reactive Plan
3. Formal and Informal Plan
4. Functional and Corporate Plan

1. Operational, Tactical and Strategic Plan

(a) ***Operational Plan:*** They are short-range plans. They are usually made in a specific and detailed manner. They provide content and form to long range plans. It is usually done at lower levels. Its primary concern is efficiency (doing things right) rather than effectiveness (doing the right things).

(b) ***Tactical (Intermediate) Plan:*** They are less detailed than the short range plans. They are concerned with implementing strategic plans by coordinating the work of different departments in the organization. Based on results obtained by implementing short-range plans, review is undertaken. The success or failure of operational plan is assessed and the need for readjustment is indicated.

(c) ***Strategic Plan (Long range plan):*** The determination of how the organizational objectives will be achieved is referred to as long range plan. Essentially, Strategy is a plan of action that will define the way in which goals can be accomplished. It links the human and other resources of an organization on the one hand, the challenges and risks posed by the outside the world on the other. The period may be five to ten years or more.

2. Proactive Vs. Reactive Plan

In proactive plan, consideration is given for the future changes and it forces the managers to be dynamic, active and creative. Managers take the initiative and attempt to shape the future and create a more desirable environment.

In reactive plan, we do not give consideration to what we desire the future to be like, to the future of the organization is left to the vagaries of social forces.

3. Formal Vs. Informal Plan

Formal plan can he defined as a written, documented plan developed through an identifiable process. The rule is that "Look before you leap".

In informal plan managers do not plan for contingencies and there is no provision for anticipate situations. They merely wait for the lightning to strike.

Formal Planning	Informal Planning
Rational	Emotional
Systematic	Disorganized
Regular intervals	Sporadic Episodes
Future Improvement	Past evaluation
Hard document	Memory

4. Corporate Plan Vs. Functional Plan

Corporate plan is integrative in nature and it has both macro and micro aspects. It takes the broad interests of the organization as a whole. It is the synthesis of various functional plans and it tries to match organizational resources with environmental opportunities/threats.

Functional plan is segmental in nature. Coordination problem often arises if production, finance, marketing and manufacturing department prepare their separate plans without a unified focus. It promotes component mentality and they fail to see the big picture and the impact of external forces on various activities of the department.

OPERATIONAL PLANNING

1. Standing/Repeated Use Plans
2. Single Use Plans

1. Standing plans

These plans are those which once formulated, they will be used for long periods and repeatedly.

(a) ***Purpose/Mission:*** Purpose is the basic intention of an organization based on which other actions are designed. It embodies the decision maker's philosophy.

(b) ***Objectives:*** They are the end results towards which activities are aimed.

(c) ***Policies:*** They are general statements/understandings, which guide thinking in a decision making, leaving it to the managers to decide within its framework.

(d) ***Procedures:*** They are guides to action rather than to thinking and indicate the exact manner in which activities must be accomplished. They are the chronological sequences of required actions.

(e) ***Rules:*** They are simplest type of plan, which prescribe in advance what is to be done or not to be done in a specific situation. It allows no scope for discretion.

(f) ***Strategy:*** It concerns with how the organization plans to meet the uncertain and competitive world outside. It is influenced by the external environment consisting of opportunities and threats and the internal environment reflects the strength and weakness of the organization.

2. Single Use Plans

(a) ***Programme:*** It is a sequence of activity to be implemented. It specifies a step-by-step approach to guide the action to achieve the goal. It assembles individual's plans and procedures and put them in a workable form to achieve the objectives.

(b) ***Project:*** A project is a small programme. Each project has a definite goal concerning task assignment and time. It is actually a proposal of investment, which can be appraised through the cost benefit analysis.

(c) ***Schedule:*** It is a process of establishing a time sequence for the work to be done. It tells us the exact time when each step would begin and when it would terminate.

(d) ***Budget:*** It is a statement of expected results in numerical terms. It may be expressed either in financial terms or in terms of labour hours, units of products, etc.

Characteristics of Effective Planning

(i) Futuristic: Planning is based on forecasting.

(ii) Primary: Planning precedes other functions of management.

(iii) Intellectual process: Planning is an intellectual process of taking decisions based on the estimated future events.

(iv) Continuity: One plan makes another plan to be followed by a series of other plans.

(v) Precision: The meaning, scope and nature of planning must be precise.

(vi) Goal oriented: Planning involves setting the objectives of an organization for achieving the target well in time.

(vii) Flexible: Planning is flexible as commitment is based on future conditions which are always dynamic.

(viii) The plan must be a sound one: It should operate in an open system approach.

(ix) Plan should reflect the needs of customers' satisfaction.

(x) There should be a monitoring system.

(xi) Plan must be simple and need based.

(xii) Planning is a continuous process.

(xiii) Planning is an interdependent process, it coordinates the activities of various departments, sections and subsections.

(xiv) Planning govern the survival, growth and prosperity of any organization.

Advantages of Planning

(i) Helps the management to implement future programmes in a systematic manner.

(ii) Facilitates the process of decision making.

(iii) Selection of optimum goals.

(iv) Meeting environmental challenges.

(v) It provides coordinated efforts and reduces risks and uncertainties.

(vi) Safeguard against business failures.

(vii) A greater utilization of resources and available facilities can be made.

(viii) Indirectly leads to large scale economies by avoiding waste of men, money, materials and machinery.

(ix) It encourages the sense of involvement and team spirit.

Limitations of Planning

(i) Time consuming and expensive.

(ii) It makes the entire organizational set up extremely rigid.

(iii) It leads to probable results and not assured goals.

(iv) It encourages a false sense of security against risk or uncertainty.

(v) Emergencies demand on the spot decision, but planning delays it.

FOR DISCUSSION

1. Define planning.
2. Explain the importance of planning.
3. Discuss the steps involved in the planning process.
4. What are the types of plan?
5. Differentiate between formal and informal plan.
6. Differentiate between standing plan and single use plan.
7. What are the characteristic features of planning?
8. Discuss the advantages and limitations of planning.

4

Decision Making Process

Managers have to take decisions all the time. They spend a lot of time in making decisions. Managers are evaluated and rewarded on the number and importance of their decisions. Decision-making is a process of thought and deliberation that leads to decisions.

Definition

Decision making is the selection based on some criteria from two/more possible alternatives. —*George R. Terry*

Decision making can be defined as the selection based on some criteria of one alternative from two/more possible alternatives. To decide means "to cut off" or in practical "to come to conclusion". —*R.S. Daver*

Characteristics of Decision making

(i) It is based on rational thinking.

(ii) It involves the evaluation of various alternatives available.

(iii) It is a process of selecting the best from among the alternatives available.

(iv) It also involves certain commitment.

(v) It is the end product because it is preceded by discussions and deliberations.

(vi) It aims to achieve organizational goals.

DECISION MAKING PROCESS

The process of decision making involves the following steps:

1. Recognizing the Problem: The first step is recognizing situations in which a decision is needed because an opportunity, a problem or a crisis exists. In most cases defining the problem is not an easy task. Opportunities and problems are not obvious. Proper emphasis on all relevant factors will greatly help in defining the problem properly and it must be realized that a problem is half solved when it is properly defined.

2. Analyzing the Problem: In this stage decision makers gather information and look for advice. He collects as many facts as he can and tries to separate facts from beliefs, opinions and preconceived notions. Each item is carefully evaluated, it is relatively weighed, its validity judged. The whole exercise helps in ensuring adequate information and essential data relating to the problem defined earlier.

3. Generating Alternatives: Normally, a business problem can be solved in many ways. If there is only one alternative, no decision is required. But in rational decision making process the manager should not jump on to any single proposal without considering all the alternatives. Decision maker searches for existing alternatives, modifies them and designs custom tailored alternatives as required, existing ones are more reliable, easier to implement and available. Koontz pointed out that the ability to develop alternatives is often as important as making a right decision among alternatives. The search for alternatives calls for creative abilities on the part of managers.

4. Evaluating the Alternatives: Here the decision maker should weigh alternative solutions against one another. All pertinent facts must be collected, they must be classified, the pros and cons must be considered and the important facts must be distinguished from trivial facts. The attempt should be to limit the alternatives to a manageable and economically feasible number.

5. Choosing the Best Alternatives: The decision maker evaluates each alternative by judging it according to some criterion (profit, cost, quality, etc). According to Drucker there are four criteria for selecting the best alternatives *viz.* risk involved, economy of effort, timing and limitation of resources.

6. Implementing and verifying the decision: Decision implementation is as important as decision formulation. A manager's decision is always a decision concerning what other people should do. Decision implementation thus includes, observing the decision as it becomes operative, modifying it when necessary, coaching the people who implement it and perfecting it once it is in action. The process of verifying is very important in the sense that it helps in highlighting the deviations and assists in taking rectificational actions in time.

DECISION MAKING TOOLS

The most important aspect of decision making is rationality. According to Simon, rationality is defined in terms of objective and intelligent action. The important aspect of rationality in decision making is maximization Vs optimization. These are two contrasting views of models of decision making with using varying degree of rationality. These models are:

1. Administrative Man Model (H.A. Simon): This model incorporates the elements of actual decision making in the real world and this theory provides a more valid prediction of the outcome to be expected from a particular manager's efforts to decide upon a course of action.

Model says that the man believes in satisfying rather than maximizing, he can make his choices without first determining all possible alternatives and without ascertaining that there are in fact all the alternatives:

Attempts to satisfy or look for the alternative which is satisfactory or good enough.

Make decisions with relatively simple rule.

2. Economic Man Model: This model is a theory of decision making under the conditions of certainty. The economic man is completely rational.

Economic man is rational in that he can order his various preferences according to his hierarchy of values and then actually makes his choice so as to maximize some desired value.

There is complete awareness of various alternatives and the outcome of each alternative can be identified so that the alternative with best outcome is chosen.

The basic difference between the economic man and administrative man model is that the former goes for searching all the alternatives and try to maximize out of his decision while in case of administrative man, he continues to reach alternatives until he finds one that meets some personally determined minimum acceptable level.

3. Group Decision-making Technique: Independent opinions and judgment are obtained again and again from members of isolated experts on a particular problem until solution is reached. Experts do not meet together so that they can avoid group conformity and problems. Process of collecting judgment and providing feedback information about others opinion is repeated several times until a consensus is reached. It is sparingly used in policy development and long range forecasting.

4. Models:

(a) ***Representation model:*** Rendering a pictorial representation and a scaled reproduction of real conditions, e.g. a road map/ Photograph.

(b) ***Analogue model:*** Using one set of properties to another set of properties, e.g. a hydraulic system using the flow of water to depict the flow of electricity.

(c) ***Mathematical/Symbolic model:*** Establish mathematical relationships between the variables of a decision problem, e.g. Mathematical formulae.

These models help in understanding, prediction involving conditions of uncertainty and risk and control of decision problems under consideration. Models are simple, convenient and relatively economic resources conservation devices for testing hypothesis-one of the most important steps in problem solving.

5. Simulation Technique: A quantitative technique for evaluating alternative courses of action based upon facts and assumptions with a computerized mathematical model in order to represent actual decision making under conditions of uncertainty.

6. Linear Programming: Dr. George D. Dantzig a mathematician who introduced his simple method—a systematic procedure for solving a linear programming problem.

How could a company with limited resources make optimum use with their resources combination for the achievement of the desired objective/goal—is the central idea of this mathematical technique. Here optimum means most profitable, least costly/concerned with least idle time for machines/men.

7. Game Theory Technique: Game theory attempts to work out optimum solution in which an individual in a given situation can develop a strategy irrespective of what a competitor does with maximizing gains or minimizing losses. It involves a highly mathematical study of tactics under conditions of uncertainty, particularly in the matter of response from the opponent (the competitor). However the technique can bring out that some tactics are more powerful and successful than others for any given game.

TYPES OF DECISIONS

1. Organizational and Personal Decisions: When a person takes a decision in the organization as an executive it will be an organizational decision. The power to take organizational decisions can be delegated from a superior to the subordinate.

An executive can also take decisions about himself. Such decisions are known as personal decisions. The power to take such decisions cannot be delegated to anybody else.

2. Routine and Strategic Decisions: Routine decisions are made repetitively following certain established rules, procedures, policies, etc. These are taken in the context of day-to-day operations of the organization and they are taken at middle and lower level management.

Strategic decisions are very important and are taken at top level management. They relate to policy matters and need the development and analysis of alternatives. These decisions influence organizational structure, objectives, working conditions, finances, etc.

3. Programmed and Non-Programmed Decisions: Programmed decisions are of a routine nature and are taken within the specified procedure. These decisions have short-term effect and are taken relatively at lower level management. The decisions to grant leave, make routine purchases, allow trade discounts, etc.

Non-repetitive decisions need arise due to specific circumstances and taken at top level management. Opening of a new branch, introducing new product, etc.

4. Individual and Group Decisions: If one person takes the decision it is known as individual decision and generally less important.

Group decisions are taken by a group of persons. The decision based on Director of committees comes under this category. The decisions are taken after a thorough discussion among persons who are assigned this work. They are generally important decisions and relate to policy matters.

Decision Support System (DSS)

Decision support system use computers to facilitate the decision making process of semi structured tasks. This system is designed not to replace managerial judgment but to support it and to make the decision process more effective. It also helps managers react quickly to changing needs. It is the design of an effective system requires a thorough knowledge of how managers make decisions.

The availability of mini computers and other computers as well as of communication networks makes it possible to access and utilize a great deal of information at low cost. Thus DSS gives managers an important tool for decision making under their own control. DSS focuses on the decision making process and on managers who, in cooperation with the technical professionals design the system suitable for a particular position. Managers, having access to data bases in DSS can manipulate data and explore the effectiveness of alternative courses of action.

Many software programmes are available for micro computers such as *Visicalc, Lotus 1-2-3 and Superlac*. There are many integrated packages, which combine programmes for word processors, spread sheets, data bases, graphics and communications with names such as *Symphony, Framework and jazz*. Thus, managers can be overwhelmed by the many choices of programmes that aid the decision making process.

Focus on semi-structured tasks requiring managerial judgment.

Emphasis on data manipulation.

Direct data access by managers.

Reliance on managers' own judgment.

Direct access to computer and data.

Manager knowing decision environment.

Emphasis on effectiveness.

Decision Tree

One of the best ways to analyze a decision is to use a so-called decision tree. It depicts in the form of a tree, the decision points, events and probabilities involved in various courses that might be undertaken. A common problem occurs in business when a new product is introduced. Managers must decide whether to install expensive permanent equipment to ensure production at the lowest possible cost or to undertake cheaper, temporary tooling that will involve a higher manufacturing cost but lower capital investment.

The decision tree approach makes it possible to see at least the major alternatives and the fact that subsequent decisions may depend on events in the future. By incorporating the probabilities of various events in the tree, managers can also comprehend the true probability of a decision's leading to desired results.

Steps Involved

(i) To plan out in a diagram form, a number of future chance events which may affect a decision.

(ii) Consider, evaluate the chance events and then arrive at a set of relative 'values' for the predicted outcome of each possible decision.

(iii) Finally choose among these outcomes, the course with highest values that is likely to produce optimum return for the company.

The main difficulty in analyzing decision tree is that even with simple two or three branch forks, the tree can become quite complex and it may run into a bush. Secondly, there is often inconsistency in assigning probabilities for different events.

FOR DISCUSSION

1. Define decision-making.
2. Discuss the characteristics of decision-making.
3. Discuss the different steps involved in decision-making process.
4. What are all the models used for decision-making?
5. Differentiate between Administrative man model and Economic man model.
6. What is DSS and discuss it?
7. Define decision tree.

5

Basic Elements and Principles of an Organization

Organizing is the larger activity of managing. It is the process, which includes:

The determination of activities necessary to accomplish the objectives.

The grouping of activities and assigning them to specified positions/persons.

The creation of network of positions/persons for managing.

Definition

Organization is to determine the activities to accomplish a job and arrange the distribution of activities among the people. —*L. Urwick*

Organization is the process of defining and grouping the activities of the enterprise and establishing the authority relationships among them. In performing the organizing function, the manager defines, departmentalizes and assigns activities so that they can be most effectively executed. —*Theo Haimann*

Organization is a process of identifying and grouping the work to be performed, defining and delegating responsibility and authority, and establishing relationships for the purpose of enabling people to work most effectively together in accomplishing objectives. —*Louis Allen*

Steps in Organization

(i) Determining the activities to be performed

(ii) Assignment of responsibilities

(iii) Delegation of authority

(iv) Selecting right men for right jobs

(v) Providing right environment

(vi) Measurement, evaluation and control.

Elements of Organizational Process

1. Departmentation: It implies the grouping of various activities on the basis of their similarity into separate units.

2. Delegation: It is the process of entrusting a part of the work by the superior to his subordinates. A manager single handedly can achieve only a few tasks hence there is need for delegation.

3. Decentralisation: It is the opposite of centralization. It refers to dispersal of decision making authority. It means that decisions are to be made by persons and at places away from the centre.

PRINCIPLES OF AN ORGANIZATION

1. Principle of Coordination: It requires that the diverse activities performed by different individuals in the organization should be properly synchronized. They should be united together in such a way as to facilitate effective accomplishment of the organizational objectives.

2. Principle of Unity of Command: An employee should receive orders and instructions from one superior only. "No man can serve two masters well". If a subordinate is answerable to more than one superior, his loyalty will be divided and there will be confusion and conflict in the organization. So dual subordination should be avoided, unless it is absolutely essential.

3. Principle of Scalar Pattern/Chain of Command: Refers to the unbroken line of authority from the top level to the bottom of an organization. Scalar chain should be clearly defined so that every subordinate knews who his superior is and to whom policy matters beyond his own authority should be referred for decisions. The line of authority is the route through which all communications are passed from the ultimate authority to the lowest ranks.

4. Principles of Definition: The duties, authority and responsibility of every individual must be clearly and precisely defined. The relations between various jobs and individuals should be defined in writing so that everybody knows what is expected of him and what are the limits of his authority. This will help to avoid confusion and overlapping of effort.

5. Principle of Exception: It implies that only those matters should be referred to higher levels of management which are of an exceptional nature or which cannot be handled effectively at lower levels. The top management should be concerned with important matters and subordinate executives should decide the routine problems. This principle makes delegation of authority really effective.

6. Principle of Objectives: Objectives should be clearly defined and fully understood by all personnel. Objectives should be laid down not only for the organization as a whole but for each department and member thereof. Lower level objectives must contribute effectively to the accomplishment of higher level objectives.

7. Principle of Authority and Responsibility: Authority and responsibility are two sides of the same coin and they should go together. Whenever a person is made responsible for something, authority should be given to him and wherever authority is delegated a person must be held responsible to it. Responsibility is absolute and a person can not escape from his responsibility by delegating his authority. Authority without corresponding responsibility results in misuse of authority, while responsibility in the absence of adequate authority leads to frustration and ineffective performance.

8. Principle of Specialization: As far as possible each individual should be given a single function or activity to perform so that he can work with greater interest and efficiency. The function or task entrusted to an individual should be appropriate to his qualifications, skills and aptitude.

9. Principle of Balance: Different departments and activities of the organization should be given a proper weightage in proportion to their contribution to the objectives. Over emphasis and under emphasis should be avoided.

10. Principle of Simplicity: The structure of the organization should be simple so that the personnel can understand assignment of duties and authority relationships.

11. Principle of Span of Control: There is a limit to the number of subordinates which a superior can effectively supervise. The limit is known as the span of control/span of management/span of supervision. The span of every manager must be proper to facilitate effective control and better performance. The span of control determines the number of levels in the organization and thereby influences the effectiveness of communication. The span of control should be legitimate (neither too wide nor too narrow) without split in the line of control.

12. Principle of Flexibility: The organizational structure should be designed as to be adjustable to the changing conditions and requirements of the enterprise.

13. Principle of Continuity: Organizing is a continuous process and the structure should be reviewed and revised regularly to keep it up-to-date and workable. It should ensure continuous growth and expansion of the business.

14. Principle of Efficiency: It is judged by its capacity to achieve the predetermined objectives at the minimum cost. The organization structure should help to satisfy the personnel and contribute to social welfare.

Concept of Responsibility, Authority and Accountability

Responsibility is the obligation of a subordinate to whom a superior has assigned a task, to perform the service as required. Duty or responsibility may be in terms of functions, targets or goals.

Responsibility is not delegatable.

Acts as a means for establishing relationships between a superior and a subordinate.

Commitment to perform the assigned tasks to the best of his/her ability.

Authority is defined as the power to make decisions, which guide actions of others. In the context of organization, authority might be termed as 'Institutionalized power'.

It rests on the chain/position. With the change in the position, the authority of individual also changes.

It is delegated to an individual by his supervisor.

It is what exists in the eye of the law.

It is the derivative of responsibility.

It serves as a basis of formal organization.

Accountability is defined as an obligation on the part of the subordinates to perform the duties. Subordinates are accountable to his superior by submission of reports from time to time. It is a derivative of authority.

Span of Management

Every person has a limited capacity to effectively supervise and control other people. No one can control an infinite number of subordinates. If a person is asked to supervise many subordinates working under him, he cannot supervise them efficiently. The capacity and ability under him is limited on account of time at his disposal, knowledge, energy, his personality, interest at other capabilities. Therefore, the number of subordinates working under him must be manageable.

Span of management refers to the optimum number of subordinates a manager can manage or control effectively.

GRAICUNAS THEORY OF SPAN OF MANAGEMENT

V.A. Graicunas, a management specialist of France has developed a mathematical formula by analyzing superior— subordinate relationship. He has identified three types of superior—subordinate relationships.

1. Direct Single Relationship: It arises from the direct and individual contacts of the superior with his subordinates. If superior has three subordinates X, Y & Z, there would be three direct single relationship.

A with X, A with Y and A with Z.

2. Direct Group Relationship: Such relationships arise between the superior and his subordinates in all possible combinations. There would be nine relationships.

A with X. Y : A with X. Z: A with X. Y & Z ....

3. Cross relationship: Refers to mutual relationships among subordinates working under a common superior. There would be 6 cross relationships.

X with Y, Y with X, Z with X, X with Z, Y with Z, Z with Y.

The number of various relationships in a particular case can be calculated with the formula

Direct single relationships = n

Direct group relationships = $n(2^{n-1} - 1)$

Cross relationships = $n(2^{n-1} + n - 1)$

where n = no. of subordinates

Graicunas has prescribed a maximum of 6 subordinates as the appropriate span of management.

TYPES OF SPAN OF MANAGEMENT

1. Narrow Span (Tall organization): Narrow span of supervision implies tall or vertical organization. Under this type of supervision, there are many levels and more supervisors are required to perform the job of guidance and control for different activities. It increases the efficiency of supervision but the cost of supervision is very high as compared to wider span of management.

2. Wider Span (Flat organization): It implies few levels of supervision. The supervisor controls and guides the activities of subordinates directly under his control. It reduces the cost of supervision.

Factors Influencing the Span of Management

(i) Capacity and ability of the superior
(ii) Competence of subordinates
(iii) Nature of work
(iv) Time available
(v) Degree available
(vi) Degree of decentralization
(vii) Quality of planning
(viii) Degree of physical fitness
(ix) Effectiveness of communication system
(x) Control mechanism

Signs of Poor Organisation

The principles should be followed by the organizations in order to meet the organizational objectives. If the organizations do not follow the principles, which are given above, they are the signs of poor organization.

FOR DISCUSSION

1. Define organizing.
2. What are the steps involved in organizing?
3. Discuss the elements of an organization.
4. What are the principles of organization?
5. Define authority, responsibility and accountability.
6. What is span of management? Explain briefly as stated by Graicunas
7. What are the different types of span of management?
8. What are the factors to be considered for span of management?

6

Departmentation and Organization Analysis

Departmentation

It is a systematic process of dividing the responsibility for operations to subordinates. It is the process of grouping employees and activities into various departments. It refers basically to horizontal differentiation in the organization.

Departmentation of the enterprise can be done by:

(i) ***Functions:*** Production, sales, finance and personnel departments.

(ii) ***Product:*** For each product or group of products, a separate department is created.

(iii) ***Territory:*** For each geographical division or territory, a separate department is created.

(iv) ***Customer:*** Departmentation by customer is followed to look after the sales function where, in the interest of efficiency and economy, special attention needs to be given to different customers.

Factors to be Considered

1. Coordination: Quite different activities may be grouped and assigned to a particular single executive in charge of a small department because they need to be coordinated for effective performance.

2. Specialization: Whatever may be the pattern of departmentation, it should be as such to field the advantage of specialization. It means proper persons must be matched with the post.

3. Significance of activities: An activity, which is considered to be the basis to the success of an enterprise, must be given proper attention. It should be assigned to a separate department at significant level of management in the overall organization.

4. Control: Departmentation is best which ensures the tight control. An activity intended to serve, as a check on another should be under a separate executive. Physical convenience of supervision should also be assigned to a separate department at significant level of management.

5. Local conditions: Management should take into consideration local condition also. They are the personalities of individuals, the nature of organization, the pattern of informal relationships in the organization, the attitude of management towards workers, the market to be served, etc.

6. Human considerations: The management should not overvalue the technical aspects of departmentation. Social aspects also have important impact on departmentation. The availability of competent managerial personnel of different levels, their attitude towards work and the managerial attitude towards personnel will also influence on the ways, the activities are departmentalized in an organization.

7. Economy: The costs to be involved in monetary and non-monetary terms both in creating a new department for any special activity should also be considered. The efficiency of the organization should not be given up for cost only. Relative efficiency and costs both should be compared.

Division of Labour

It is the root of any organizational structure. In order to improve the efficiency of any organization, the total efforts of persons who joined together for common purpose have to be divided into different functions. These functions are further divided into sub-functions, each to be performed by different persons. After the division of the total effort into functions and sub functions, the next step is to group the activities on the basis of similarity of work for e.g., in a manufacturing enterprise, its total activities may be divided and grouped under (a) production, (b) Marketing, (c) Finance and (d) Personnel.

Even within each of these groups or departments, one or more sub-departments or sections may be created to look after particular activities.

Placement

The process of placing the right man for the right job is called placement. A worker should be placed in a position based on his strengths.

ORGANIZATION CLIMATE, ORGANIZATIONAL DECISIONS AND ORGANIZATIONAL ANALYSIS

Types of Organization

1. Formal Organization: It refers to the structure of well-defined jobs, definite measure of authority, responsibility and accountability. The structure is consciously designed to enable the people of the organization to work together for accomplishing common objectives.

It is deliberately impersonal

It is based on ideal relationship

It is based on rabble hypothesis of the nature of man

Bureaucratic and red tapism

2. Informal Organization: It refers to the relationship between people in the organization based on personal attitudes, emotions, prejudices, likes and dislikes, etc. These relations are not developed according to procedures and regulations laid down in the formal organization structure. Generally large formal groups give rise to small informal or social groups. These groups may be based on same taste, language, culture or any other factor. These groups are not preplanned but they develop automatically within the organization, e.g. music club, sports, politics, etc.

Organizational Structure

Organization structure refers to the formal pattern or network of vertical and horizontal authority relationships among different positions in an enterprise and among the personnel occupying these positions. There is no ideal structure of organization relationships, which can suit all enterprises. There are several types of organizational structures, each reflecting a particular pattern of authority relationships.

1. Line Organization: It is the basic framework for the whole organization. It represents a direct vertical relationship through which authority flows. This is the simplest and oldest form of internal organization. This is also known as scalar organization. The authority flows from the top to the lower level. The organization is vertical structure where one person delegates authority to his subordinates and who in turn delegate to his subordinates and so on. Authority flows vertically and from top persons to all persons responsible for execution of work. Since the authority and responsibility flow in an unbroken straight line, it is called the line organization.

Merits

(i) It is simple to establish and can be easily understood by the employees.

(ii) It helps in fixing authority and responsibility of each and every person in the organization.

(iii) The hierarchy in management helps in achieving effective coordination.

(iv) There is effective communication.

(v) Easy to operate and less expensive.

(vi) Effective control and supervision.

(vii) It is flexible since the manager has to take all-important decisions, he can make changes if new situation warrants.

Drawbacks

(i) It has centralized decision.

(ii) Lack of specialization.

(iii) Overloading of duties.

(iv) Lack of communication.

(v) Red tapism and bureaucracy.

2. Line and Staff Organization: In this type of organization structure, there are two types of relationships. Line relationship is a decision maker and staff person is an advisor.

Line refers to those positions and elements of organization, which have the responsibility and authority and are accountable for the accomplishment of primary objectives. Staff elements who have responsibility and authority for providing advice and service to the line in the attainment of objectives. *–Allen*

Merits

(i) There is planned specialization.

(ii) There is a well-defined authority and responsibility. The line of command is maintained.

(iii) The staff with its expert knowledge provides opportunities to the line officers for adopting a rational multi-dimensional view towards a problem.

(iv) It nourishes organization growth as each man grows in his own specialty. It also helps coordination through cooperation and leadership.

Drawbacks

(i) Conflict between line and staff organization.
(ii) Lack of responsibility on the part of staff specialist.
(iii) Absence of thinking on the part of line staff.
(iv) Expensive.

3. Functional Organization: In this type of organization there are number of specialists, each having authority over a particular function or a group of related functions throughout the organization. Each specialist has a control over the function under his charge, no matter where that function is performed in the organization. He controls all the individuals working in that functional area. For instance, a human resource department would recruit, train and develop people required for all other departments of the organization. Functional organization can be used at higher levels as well as lower levels of management. Each functional head issues orders throughout the organization with respect to the function.

Merits

(i) There is a complete specialization of work and every worker receives expert guidance of several specialists.
(ii) As each supervisor is an expert in his area of work, supervision and control are likely to be better.
(iii) There is democratic control.
(iv) The growth and expansion of the enterprise is not limited to the capabilities of few line managers.

Drawbacks

(i) Complex.
(ii) Coordination problem.
(iii) It weakens disciplinary control by making workers to work under different works.

Differences between Line, Line and Staff and Functional Organization

S.No.	Criteria	Line Organization	Line and Staff Organization	Functional Organization
1.	Nature	Simple and operate	Complex	More complex
2.	Suitability	Small enterprise	Medium and large	Very large

3.	Work load of manager	Overload	Relief	Some over work and some relief
4.	Speciali-zation	Moderate/ small degree of specialization	High degree	Still high degree
5.	Unity of command	Strictly observed	Observed	Violated
6.	Economy	Economical to introduce	Expensive	More expensive

4. Matrix Organization: Matrix or grid organization is a hybrid structure combining two complementary structures— functional departmentation with pure project structure. Functional structure is a permanent feature of the matrix organization and retains authority for the overall operation of the functional units. Project departments are created whenever specific projects require a high degree of technical skill and the other resources for a temporary period. Functional departments create a vertical chain of command while the project team forms the horizontal lines, thereby forming a matrix.

A matrix organization is a two-dimensional structure, a combination of pure project structure and the traditional functional departments. It has been developed to meet the need of large and complex organizations, which require a structure more flexible and technically oriented rather than the functional structures.

Merits

(i) It helps to focus attention to talent and resources on a single project which facilitates better planning and control.

(ii) It is more flexible than the traditional functional structures.

(iii) It provides an environment in which professionals can test their competence and make maximum contributions.

5. Project Organization: It is set up with the objective of overcoming the major weaknesses of the functional organization, namely, absence of unity of command, delay in decision making and lack of coordination. A project organization can also be the beginning of an organization. The project may become a long term or permanent effort that eventually becomes a programme (branch) organization. Later it may get separated from the parent organization and be established as a full-fledged product division functionally organized.

6. Committee Organization: A committee means a group of persons formed for a special purpose. According to Davis a committee is group of individuals who meet for the purpose of effecting an integration of ideas concerning a solution for some problems.

(i) *Advisory Committee:* are the staff committees and play the advisory role of assisting the line executives. Advisory committees probe a given problem or issue for the line executive. It collects all the necessary information, analyses it after scrutinizing the problem from all possible angles, arrives at conclusions on the basis of which it sends a report to line executive, with recommendations for a course of action.

(ii) *Executive Committee:* have the executive power of decision making, policy forming, organizing, directing and controlling the activities. Such committees are set up at the top level of the organization.

Direction

Direction is the essence of all operations in an organization. It is defined as the process of supervising, guiding, leading, motivating and communicating the human factor to achieve organizational objectives.

Supervision

The aim of supervision is to ensure that subordinates work efficiently to accomplish the tasks assigned to them.

The lowest level managers are designated as supervisors. One reason for this is that while all other levels of management have subordinates who are managers themselves, the supervisory staff deals with workers who are engaged in basic operations.

Qualities of a Good Supervisor

(i) Knowledge about the organization
(ii) Technical competency
(iii) Ability to instruct and explain
(iv) Ability to listen to others to get information, to solve problems, to share experiences, etc.
(v) Ability to secure co-operation
(vi) Ability of orderly thinking
(vii) Ability to judge people
(viii) Patience
(ix) Ability to improve worker's morale
(x) Ability to delegate the work among his subordinates

Guiding

It refers to a specialized task of leading the subordinates to accomplish the result by overcoming the hurdles. Direction and purpose are very important for a manager to his subordinate.

Leadership

It is the ability of a supervisor to influence the behaviour of his subordinates and persuade them to follow a particular course of action.

Functions of a Leader

(i) Executive
(ii) Planner
(iii) Policy maker
(iv) Expert
(v) External group representative
(vi) Controller of internal relations
(vii) Conveyor of rewards and punishments, and
(viii) Arbitrator and mediator.

Types of Leader

(i) ***Autocratic*** wants to run show all by himself.

(ii) ***Laissez faire*** or free rein leaders permits his followers to do whatever they want to do.

(iii) ***Institutional Leader*** is one who wields power over his followers due to the position or office occupied by him in the organizational hierarchy.

Differences between Autocratic and Democratic Leader

S. No.	Authoritative/Autocratic	Participative/Democratic
1.	Exhibiting the style of Theory X leader	Exhibiting the style of Theory Y leader
2.	Leader is task oriented and restrictive	Follower oriented and permission
3.	One way communication	Two way communication
4.	Decision making is centralized and quick decisions are taken	Decentralized decision making and slow process of making decision
5.	Winning over employee confidence is difficult	Leader gains a contended and cohesive group confidence

(iv) ***Democratic*** leadership is based on the assumption that the leader derives his power by the consent of the followers. Participation, consultation and agreement of the group members are important features of democratic leadership.

(v) ***Expert or Functional Leader*** does not have any formal authority. He stands out because of his special qualifications for the job handled by him, which is also the main reason why followers look up to him for guidance and control.

Qualities of Leadership

According to Henry Fayol the qualities of leader are:

(i) Health and physical fitness
(ii) Mental vigour and energy
(iii) Courage to accept responsibility
(iv) Steady, persistent, thoughtful determination
(v) Sound general education
(vi) Management ability embracing foresight and the art of handling men
(vii) Sense of judgment
(viii) Understanding or empathy
(ix) Motivation
(x) Communication skill.

FOR DISCUSSION

1. What is departmentation?
2. What are the factors to be considered for departmentation?
3. What is division of labour?
4. Define organization structure.
5. What are line, line and staff and functional organization?
6. Differentiate between line, line and staff and functional organization.
7. What are matrix, project and committee organization?
8. What is direction?
9. Define leader and types of leader.
10. Differentiate between autocratic leader and democratic leader.
11. What are the qualities and functions of leadership?

7

Delegation—Concept and Principles

Delegation is an important managerial practice of getting things done through other people by sharing authority with them. In any typical organization, the Board of Directors takes the policy and strategic decisions and actual implementation of these is entrusted to the chief executive. However, the chief executive alone cannot do the entire work. He cannot even supervise the work of all individuals working in different departments. He can pass on some portions of his authority to different departmental managers and commit them to specific tasks of supervision and operation. This process is known as delegation of authority.

Definition

Delegation means assigning work to others and giving them authority to do it. —*F.G. Moore*

Delegation means conferring authority from one executive or organizational unit to another in order to accomplish particular assignment. —*George R. Terry.*

Nature of Delegation

(i) Delegation is not abdication.
(ii) Delegation is not abandonment.
(iii) Delegation does not mean to avoid decisions.
(iv) Delegation is an act or a process.
(v) It refers to relationship between two individuals *i.e.* a superior and his immediate subordinates.

Need of Delegation

Delegation of authority is widely recognized as an art of getting best results. It reduces the burden of top executives by relieving them of the botheration of taking routine decisions. In general the significance of delegation can be summarized as

(i) Delegation leads to better decisions.
(ii) It relieves the manager from heavy workload.
(iii) It speeds up decision making.
(iv) It helps to improve the motivation and morale of subordinates.
(v) It facilitates training of subordinates.
(vi) It creates a formal organization structure.
(vii) It provides continuity.
(viii) It improves behavioural climate.

PRINCIPLES OF DELEGATION

1. Principle of Functional Definition: This principle states that every job must carry a job description. In the absence of a well-defined job description, there arise confusion about the performance of the job. The content of each position, the duties involved, the authority-responsibility contemplated and the relationships with other positions should be clearly defined in writing and made known to all concerned.

2. Principle of Delegation by Results Expected: The authority should be delegated to the extent and in the manner necessary to show results. It presupposes that goals have been made, that they are communicated and understood and the jobs have been set up to fit in with them.

3. Scalar Principle: It states that supreme authority vests at the top. There is a clear line of flow of authority to the lower levels. Every subordinate must know who delegates' authority to him and to whom matters beyond his own authority must be referred.

4. Authority Level Principle: It states that the subordinate to whom authority is delegated should make the decision himself and only exceptional things and decisions are to be referred upward. It means the principle of exception. Only those decisions are to be referred upward which cannot be made within the scope of the authority delegated.

5. Principle of Unity of Command: It states that a subordinate will report to a single superior. It is also called as the principle of single accountability. Authority should flow from single superior to subordinate because serving two superiors will create confusion and conflicts.

6. Principle of Absoluteness of Responsibility: The responsibility of superior for the acts of his subordinates is absolute. Similarly, the responsibility of a subordinate to his superior is also absolute once he has accepted an assignment and the authority to carry it out.

7. Principle of Parity of Authority and Responsibility: Responsibility should be the same as the authority delegated. A man should not be held responsible for something over which he had no formal authority and to control and exercise of formal authority, a man should be answerable for his actions. There is always equity of authority and responsibility.

LIMITATIONS OF DELEGATION

There are many difficulties in delegating authority in an organization. Those difficulties may be grouped into three categories, which are as follows:

1. On the Part of the Organization

(i) Inadequate planning.
(ii) Lack of effective control mechanism.
(iii) Defective organization structure and non-clarity of relationships.
(iv) Violation of unity of command principle.

2. On the Part of the Superior

(i) Lack of ability in direction.
(ii) Lack of willingness to test subordinates.
(iii) Lack of willingness to give subordinates a chance.
(iv) Lack of setting control standards for subordinates.
(v) Fear of competition.

3. On the Part of Subordinates

(i) Lack of self-confidence.
(ii) Lack of incentives.
(iii) Overburdened with work.
(iv) Subordinates preference to depend on superior rather than to take decisions themselves.
(v) Fear of criticism.
(vi) Lack of information and resources to use the authority and achieve desired results.

WAYS OF GIVING GOOD DIRECTION

The three main techniques of direction that the manager makes use of are: consultative or participative, Let go and Autocratic methods.

1. Consultative/Participative: The essential feature of this method is that the executive discusses the problem with his subordinates, invites their opinions and suggestions and takes them into consideration before taking decisions and issuing necessary directives for carrying them out. This develops competency and a sense of responsibility in the subordinates.

Merits

(i) Better decisions through shared information.
(ii) Relationship between the manager and subordinates is good.
(iii) High satisfaction and decreased dependence on the leader.
(iv) Defensiveness on the part of employees is reduced.

2. Let go/Laissez faire: This technique of direction induces the subordinates to make use of their own initiative, encourages creative thinking, drive and intelligence in the solution of problems. The superior remains watchful to see that the activities of the subordinates are directed rightly to achieve the desired objectives. He also keeps himself readily available for any consultation the subordinates may need.

3. Autocratic: This method completely takes away the room for discretion or initiative by the subordinates. Whatever they are required to do and even the manner in which they have to do it—all these are laid down to the minute details in the order from the superior. Superior always prefers to do everything himself. Subordinates would blindly follow the instructions of the boss irrespective of the consequences. If anything goes wrong, the superior will be answerable for it.

Merits

(i) The decisions are very speedy.
(ii) Most suited at the time of crisis or when the subordinates are efficient.

Demerits

(i) Subordinates are compelled to follow directions of the leader even though they may be wrong.
(ii) If the leader is weak and inefficient the followers also be weak and inefficient.

FOR DISCUSSION

1. What is delegation?
2. Need and nature of delegation in an organization.
3. Explain the important principles of delegation with example.
4. Discuss the limitations of delegation in organization.
5. What are the ways of giving good direction in an organization?

8

Coordination and Control

Coordinating is a by-product of directing. It is a key function of the executive and a continuous concern of top management. Coordination is the effort to ensure the smooth interplay of the functions and forces of all the different components and parts of an organization to the end that its purpose will be realized with a minimum of friction and minimum of collaborative effectiveness. Coordination is the substance of management. Managing an organization is an impossible task without proper coordination among various parts. Without coordination, the activities represent disjoined pieces placed together and the output of the organization will be nil if not negative.

Definition

Coordination is the balancing and keeping the team together by ensuring a suitable allocation of working activities to the various members and seeing that they are performed with due harmony among the members themselves.

—*F.L. Brech*

Coordination is defined as a process by which group efforts are made in orderly sequence and unity of action is ensured in the pursuit of a common objective.

Cooperation

It refers to the collective efforts of people who associate voluntarily to achieve specified objectives. It indicates merely the willingness of individuals to help each other and it is the result of voluntary attitude of the people. It provides the foundation for coordination by enlisting voluntary efforts. Cooperation is a necessary but not a sufficient condition of coordination.

S. No.	Coordination	Cooperation
1.	Deliberate and conscious effort of the people	Voluntary attitude of a group of people
2.	Requires concurrence of purpose, harmony of effort and concerted action	Willingness of individuals to help each other

PRINCIPLES OF COORDINATION

The principles, which form the basis of successful coordination are as follows:

1. Direct Contact: Coordination to be effective must be through direct correspondence or personal contact. Every enterprise needs a horizontal relationship among the workers. With the free exchange of ideas between the people concerned, the way is smoothened for understanding and mutual confidence. That way many problems could be satisfactorily solved at lower levels instead of being referred to senior executives.

2. Groundwork: Coordination is not something to be done as a follow up. It must form a part of the early stages of planning and policy making. Planning without taking into account the aspects of coordination will lead to unnecessary trouble and wastage of efforts.

3. Continuity: Coordination should be a continuous process. The need for it does not end once the establishment starts running. Beginning at the planning stage, coordination runs through the functions of organizing, directing and controlling.

4. Integration: Coordination should aim at an integral whole, reconciling different and conflicting interests or ideas or approaches that are bound to be there in any human organization.

5. Self-coordination: This principle states that when a particular department affects the functions of other department, the affected department may not be having control over other department, for e.g., there must be coordination between the level of production and sales. When the production department alters its total production in such a way as to suit the sales capacity of the marketing department (even before the marketing department makes request to cut down production or to increase production) then self-coordination is said to have taken place. This, of course, requires effective communication across the department.

STEPS INVOLVED IN COORDINATION PROCESS

Coordination involves a series of deliberate steps, which include the following:

1. Clarifying Authority and Responsibility: Clear demarcation of functions and the powers and the responsibilities that go with them will prevent overlapping of authority, which breeds most problems of coordination.

2. Checking, Observation and Guidance: These are control measures. The executive here is not to remain as a spectator just watching the show, he must check and find out how far the efforts at coordination have succeeded. In this process, the executive takes notice of the actions of his subordinates, particularly those actions that still appear to be uncoordinated with consequent maladjustments in operations. The executive, while studying these reports, will come across the factors that prevent coordination at one phase or the other and then he can take steps to set them right.

3. Decision-making System: Design of a decision-making system such that managers monitor the organizational activity personally and otherwise, perceive problems of coordination and quickly find solution with a situational perspective.

4. Effective Communication: It is important for ensuring coordination. Special committees formed for this purpose, staff meetings at regular intervals and personal contacts are the main communication channels, in the context of coordination.

5. Quality Leadership: Coordination cannot be achieved without effective leadership. In fact the very success of a leadership signifies the extent of coordination achieved so far as the group effort is concerned.

6. Reward System: Development of a rational and feasible reward system both monetary and non-monetary—such that people respond by complying with the required performance and behavioural standards.

METHODS OF COORDINATION

1. Personal Mode: Direct contact between managers and employees or through officer or through feed back systems.

2. Impersonal Mode: Standardization of operating procedures (SOPs), plans and schedules.

3. Group Mode: By committee, task force, meetings, coordination department, etc.

Controlling

Controlling is the integral part of managerial process. It is a monitoring function of ascertaining whether organizational efforts are heading towards the stated objectives or not. The managerial function of controlling is mainly concerned with measuring and recording variations in performance and taking necessary corrective actions for the future.

Definition

Controlling Is checking current performance against predetermined standard contained in the plans, with a view to ensuring adequate progress and satisfactory performance, also recording the experience gained from the working of these plans as a guide to possible future operations.

—F.L. Brech

Controlling may be defined as comparing results with the plans and taking corrective actions when the results deviate from the plans.

Nature/Characteristics of Control

(i) Control is a dynamic process. It involves continuous review of standards of performance and results in corrective action, which may lead to changes in other functions of management.

(ii) It is a continuous activity.

(iii) It is a function of management and it is a follow up action to other functions of management.

(iv) It is a pervasive function *i.e.* performed by all the managers in the organization to control the activities assigned to them.

(v) Control is forward looking. It is related to future, as past cannot be controlled.

(vi) It is usually preventive as the presence of control systems leads to minimize wastages, losses and deviations from the standard.

(vii) The essence of control is action. The performance of control is achieved only when the corrective action is taken on the basis of feedback information.

(viii) Planning and control are closely related.

Importance of Controlling

(i) To ensure that activities are performed in accordance with the predetermined standard that is to see that activity is achieving the desired result.

(ii) To know what is happening or what has actually happened in the organization.

(iii) To determine the corrective action, if any, required for the achievement of goals with a minimum of time, effort and expense.

(iv) To co-ordinate the diverse activities and efforts.

(v) To improve the efficiency of operations by minimizing unnecessary and wasteful actions.

(vi) Good controls in fact lead to greater organizational effectiveness.

Methods of Controlling

There are different methods of control systems. From these methods we get to know and can measure how well organization goals and plans have been executed. Those important methods are:

1. Production Control: This is concerned with the products that are being manufactured. It is the process of planning production in advance of operations, establishing the exact route of each individual item, part or assembly, setting, starting and finishing dates for each important item and realizing the necessary orders as well as initiating the required follow up to the effect that of the smooth functioning of the enterprise.

2. Budgetary Control: A budget is a financial plan for a definite period of time. This control evolves a course of action that would make the realization of the budgeted targets possible.

3. Inventory Control: It refers to controlling the kind, amount, location, movement and timing of the various commodities used in and produced by the enterprises.

4. Cost Control: It refers to control of all the costs of an undertaking both direct and indirect in order to achieve cost effectiveness in business operations.

5. Quality Control: This system while exercising quality control over the products being manufactured makes use of statistical quality control techniques. To help assure satisfactory quality, both quality control and inspection are employed. Statistical quality control is based on the statistical theories and methods of probability to sample testing from work in process.

6. External and Internal Audit Control: External audit is enforced by law in respect of all joint stock companies, cooperatives etc. Its objective is to safeguard the interest of the shareholder against the malpractice of management.

Firms may also have internal audit under which staff members of the company may verify financial transactions and financial record for analyzing the overall control system of the organization.

7. Profit and Loss Control: Profit and loss control refers to a control system under which sales, expenses and profits of each branch or division are compared with those of other branches and divisions as well as with historical trends with a view to measuring deviations and taking necessary corrective action.

8. Authority Control: This system prescribes jurisdiction and limits of authority that can be exercised by personnel placed at different levels in an organizational set up. Job descriptions and policy directives generally serve as guidelines in this direction.

Liaison of Manager

Manager must possess the following attributes:

(i) He should have faith in the capacity of people to change and develop at any stage of their life.

(ii) He should have constant desire to learn and develop himself. Some common ways are reading, experimenting, sharing experiences with others, attending conferences and visiting other organizations.

(iii) He should have extension motivation *i.e.* a desire to help others. He should be prepared to sacrifice his own personal goals for group goals.

(iv) He should possess good communication skill to sell his ideas to others in the organization.

(v) He should be good listener.

(vi) He should be proactive, *i.e.* he should take initiative in introducing and implementing new ideas.

(vii) He should have enough patience to wait till his actions bear fruit.

(viii) He should be free from bias.

(ix) He should have leadership qualities. He should be able to lead by personal example so that his preaching to others has credibility.

(x) He should have respect for and knowledge of others' functions in the organization.

(xi) He should have knowledge and understanding of individual and group behaviour.

(xii) He should have professional knowledge of the various activities of the organization.

FOR DISCUSSION

1. Define Coordination.
2. Differentiate between coordination and cooperation.
3. Discuss the principles of coordination in organization.
4. Discuss the steps involved in coordination process.
5. What are the methods of coordination?
6. What is controlling?
7. Discuss the nature and importance of controlling in organization.
8. Discuss the different types of control.
9. Discuss the liaison of manager.

9

Budgeting and Auditing

Among the several techniques of managerial control, budgeting is one and it is a statement of anticipated results expressed in numerical terms. It is prepared in advance of the period to which it applies. It is an instrument of planning as well as control. Budgeting is the process of preparing budgets.

Definition

Budget is a financial and or quantitative statement prepared prior to a definite period of time, of the policy to be pursued during that period for the purpose of attaining a given objective.

Budget is an estimate of future needs arranged according to an orderly basis, covering some or all of the activities of an enterprise for a definite period of time.

Budgetary Control

Budgetary control is a process of finding out what is being done and comparing the actual results with the corresponding budget data in order to approve accomplishments by either adjusting the budget estimates or correcting the cause of differences. —*George R. Terry*

Budgetary control involves the use of budgets and budgetary reports throughout the period to coordinate, evaluate and control day-to-day operations in accordance with the goal specified by the budget.

—*Glen A. Welsch*

Purpose of Budgeting

(i) To lay down business policies for the achievement of desired objectives during a certain period of time. Budgetary control provides definite targets.

(ii) To coordinate the diverse activities and efforts in the organization so that policies are successfully executed.

(iii) To regulate the activities and efforts of people to ensure that the actual results conform to the planned results.

(iv) To efficient use of human and physical resources.

(v) Budgets serve as strong incentives to employees by laying down targets of performance.

(vi) Budgeting facilitates delegation of authority because a budget provides automatic sanction for execution of work.

TYPES OF BUDGET

1. Master Budget: This is an overall budget for the organization as a whole. It is prepared by consolidating departmental or functional budgets and its purpose is to coordinate departmental activities.

2. Functional Budgets: Functional budgets may be of the following types:

(a) *Production budget:* The production budget contains the manufacturing programmes of the enterprise. It defines the plant capacity, stock limits, quantity and the quality of production of different products. It is helpful in estimating the cost of production. This budget is often divided into several budgets.

(i) Material budget, which specifies the quantity, quality and cost of materials, required for uninterrupted production.

(ii) Labour budget, which lays down the requirements for labour in terms of the number and type of workers for different jobs.

(iii) Plant and equipment budget which defines the requirements of machines, equipments and tools including their repairs and maintenance.

(iv) Research and development budget, which lays down the estimated cost on research and development for creating new products and for improving existing products.

(b) *Financial budget:* This budget reveals the estimates of the capital required for both long term and short-term needs of the enterprise at different points of time in future. An important part of this budget is the cash budget, which contains estimated receipts and payments of cash over the specified future period. It helps to detect possible shortages or excess of cash in the business. The financial budget also contains estimates of the firm's profits and expenditure *i.e.* the operating budget (Goods and services the organization expects to consume in a budget period).

(c) ***Sales budget:*** The sales budget is an estimate of total sales revenue and selling expenses of the firm. It is based upon information relating to past sales, degree of competition, sales potential, etc. The sales budget serves as the basis of other functional budgets. The sales budget may be broken area wise or product wise.

(d) ***Overheads budget:*** An estimate of factory overheads, distribution costs and administrative heads is known as the over heads budget. The capital expenditure budget contains a forecast of the capital investment.

BUDGETING PROCESS

The process of budgeting consists of the following steps:

1. Budgetary Objectives: Budgets are a means to certain ends. Hence the objectives to be achieved during a certain period of time should be defined clearly and precisely before preparing budgets. Those responsible for the preparation and implementation of budgets must understand fully the objectives and policies of the organization.

2. Budgetary Organization: Budgets are prepared and used through organizational relationships. Departmental managers are given the authority to prepare functional budgets. The chief executive is responsible for the coordination of different budgets.

3. Budget Centers: A budget center is an organizational unit established for cost control. All budgets should be linked with cost centers so that the responsibility for budgeting and results can be fixed.

4. Budget Controller: A special officer is appointed for the administration of budgets. He provides valuable advice and assistance in the preparation, execution, coordination and revision of business budgets. The budget controller also gives warning of deviations from the budgeted performance.

5. Budget Committee: A budget committee consisting of various executives is constituted to assist the budget controller. The chief executive serves as the chairman and this committee approves the functional budgets or sends them for revision to the departmental heads. The budget committee helps in securing participation of personnel in the preparation and administration of budgets.

6. Budget Period: A budget is prepared for a specific period of time in the future. The period or duration of the budget should be determined according to the circumstances of the organization. The budget period should correspond with the natural cycle of business.

7. Budget Manual: A budget manual is a document containing the forms and records required for budgetary control. It serves as a guide to executives in the preparation and administration of budgets.

AUDITING

Auditing is the process of appraisal and it is associated with detecting fraud. It has many uses, from validating the honesty and fairness of financial statements for providing a critical basis for management decisions.

External Auditing

It is largely a verification process involving the independent appraisal of the organization's financial accounts and statements. Assets and liabilities are verified and financial reports are checked for completeness and accuracy. The audit is conducted by accounting personnel employed by an outside firm or by chartered accountants. -

It plays a significant role in encouraging honesty, not only in the preparation of statements, but also in the actual operation of the organization. External audit takes place after the organization's operating period is finished and its financial statements are completed. It does not usually make a major contribution to control of the ongoing operations of the organization.

Internal Auditing

The internal audit is carried out by members of the organization. Its objective is to provide reasonable assurance that the assets of the organization are being properly safeguarded and the financial records are being kept reliably and accurately enough for the preparation of financial statements. It concentrates on the operations of the organization and this is known as 'operational auditing'.

Computer Aided Planning and Budgeting

Use of computers in the preparation of plans and budgets is called computer aided planning and budgeting.

Computer is the greatest tool ever invented by man, since it amplifies the capacity of man's most important possession, the brain. It has the power as a tool to extend the capacity of human brain. The computer is making fundamental changes and quantum improvement in all the important inventions made earlier by man and hence it is in a class by itself. High speed, great accuracy, a large storage capacity, extreme compactness, high reliability and unusual versatility are the special features of modern computer.

As far as applications are concerned, computers are capable of functioning at different levels of complexity, using the special feature. The simplest level is the mechanization of manual operations and routine work. They do simple data processing, arithmetical and logical operations. Many business applications are at this level of complexity. At the second level of complexity there are decision and control operations. In such applications, computers are used for controlling operations or for helping in in decision and control applications. In such applications, the computer, makes use of a wide range of techniques like statistical methods, operations research, simulation and so on. At this level of Complexity, we can have good information storage and retrieval. The next higher level of application which is still being developed concerns machine intelligence, robotics, natural language processing, playing games and expert systems are few examples of the machine intelligence concept. Most of the applications described above are fully implemented in advanced countries. There is hardly any field where computers have not been used.

In agriculture, computer-based research produces new yielding varieties of plants. In developed countries, there are farms functioning by remote control. A program for crop growing controls the planting and determines the fertilizer needed. When compared to other field, agriculture has not adequately utilized the opportunities developed by the computer revolution. However, a conceptual view is drawn in the paper about the major issues and applications of computer in Agriculture planning and budgeting.

Areas of Computer Aided Planning and Budgeting:

(i) Receipt and Expenditure accounts details of a concern.

(ii) Pay roll.

(iii) Inventory control of the stocks and various plants for effective production control.

(iv) PERT/CPM techniques of project management.

(v) Operation Research application for planning process.

(vi) Agricultural Information system.

(vii) Rainfall prediction.

(viii) Pest and Disease monitoring system.

(ix) Computer Aided Design of Agricultural Machinery.

(x) Artificial Intelligence system for Agriculture.

Hardware Components

Basic need for using computer for agricultural application is computer hardware. The minimum need is a PCXT with 20-MB hard disk, 640 KB main memory and 1x1.2-MB floppy disk drive with a monitor and a graphics printer.

Software Components

The following are the minimum requirements of software for different applications:

1. MS-DOS	- To make the computer work
2. Word star	- Preparation of scientific and other document
	- Acts as an editor for FORTRAN Programme
3. FORTRAN/BASIC	- To solve the problems
4. AutoCAD	- To prepare machine drawings
	- Design and drafting application
	- Simulation studies
	- 2D/3D - isometric drawings
	- Viewing of drawing in different rotation, angles, etc.
5. Lotus/Harvard Graphics	- Spread sheet application
6. Dbase/FoxBASE/FoxPro	- Creation of data base
	- Sorting, printing and computing
	- Program for formulation

Liveware Components

Any scientific person with minimum knowledge of logistic can easily learn and use the computer. Hence, the agricultural graduates working in the State Departments can easily be trained on Computer for Farm Planning and Budgeting.

Planning in Agriculture

(i) ***Rainfall Prediction:*** The rainfall, temperature, relative humidity at different zones has to be stored in the computer. A package has to use these upto data and predict the rainfall and other climatic parameters for the next season. Based on this, the crop planning can be made so as to fetch maximum income to farmers. Tamil Nadu Agricultural University has made some headway in this direction of rainfall prediction and contingency crop planning.

(ii) ***Pest and Disease Monitoring:*** The type of pest/disease, quantum of incidents, level of damage to a particular crop and its relevant relative parameters like temperature, sunshine hours, humidity and rainfall has to be stored in computer. A viable computer package has to be developed to predict such pest and disease information system so as to make necessary plant protection measures in time.

(iii) ***Agricultural Information Bank:*** Details like quantum of crop produced, area of cultivation, type of terrain and suitable crop details can be stored into computer so that its retrieval is easier and many people can share this information. The various components of Agricultural Information Bank are:

Soil information | Crop information
Weather information | Pest and Disease information.

Development of Planning System

The following figure will give us how a system is conceived for development:

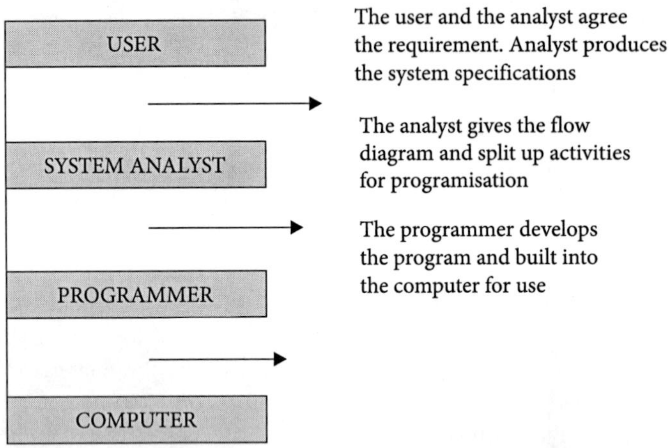

Fig. 1. Interaction of system analyst with user for system development

(i) ***Terms of Reference:*** Computer application in various activities of an organization is essential task so that the organization can cope up with its commitment to complete the objectives. Administration and the various users of the organization have to come up to a conclusion about which part of the activity has to be computerized and to what extent. The terms and conditions, the responsibility and decountability have to be clearly spelled out.

(ii) ***Project Feasibility:*** The system analyst has to interact with the users and has to prepare a detailed feasibility report. The analyst should specify what would be the advantages/ disadvantages of computerizing an activity and the extent of financial commitment. The project should be technically feasible and economically viable one. If the system is accepted by the firm for computerization, then the detailed system study has to be taken up.

(iii) ***Full System Study:*** The various components of a system study are:

Fact finding

Recording

Analysis

Statement of requirement

The analyst has to study the manual system by having direct discussion with the various people involved in an activity. All facts have to be recorded, analyzed. Keeping in view the minimum requirement expected from the system as the future requirements various alternate ways have to be thought of and finally come to a new improved system.

(iv) ***Programme Specifications:*** The analyst has to develop suitable programme flow chart and system flow chart and pass on the information to a programmer. The programmer develops the programme for successful execution.

(v) ***System Testing:*** The collection of various programmes and data files developed for a particular application is tested for normal input data and also analysed.

(vi) ***Documentation:*** System development is a costly affair, it is done by investing the manpower and the costly machine power. Whatever the programmes developed, it has to be fully supported by written documentation. Staffs working in any organization are subject to change but the organization will be there forever. Hence, the future of this organization is fully depending on properly developed, codified and classified documents.

(vii) ***System Implementation:*** After testing of the system, ..it has to be implemented for life 'activities. During the implementation stage, the unexpected and unplanned things will normally happen. These difficulties have to be diagnosed and should be removed one after the other, so that the programmes developed should work for the life data and should yield and desire results.

(viii) ***System maintenance:*** The programme and data collected/ developed have to be carefully protected from its various users. Data corruption due to power failures has to be minimized by efficient hardware management. Timely back up and restricted movements of computer operation and programmes will solve the problems to some extent.

(ix) ***Conclusion:*** The role of Computer, the minimum requirement of hardware, software and liveware for project planning for an agricultural development office in a block level were indicated. The issues connected with the development of planning system for agricultural packages were also summarized.

Zero Based Budgeting (ZBB)

ZBB is a relatively new approach to budgeting for general administrative costs, special programmes or clearly identifiable projects. The key element of ZBB is future objective orientation of past objectives. Instead of taking last year's budget and adjusting them for finding out the future level of activity and preparation of budgets, ZBB forces management to review the current ongoing objective and operations.

ZBB is a type of budget that requires managers to rejustify the past objectives, projects and budgets and to set priorities for the future. ZBB differs from traditional budgeting and here the manager without referring to the past priorities recalculate the estimate for all the organizational activities and decides which should be eliminated or funded at reduced level or current level or increased level.

Steps Involved in ZBB

(i) ***Decision package:*** Each discrete department activity and programme is broken down into a decision package. It summarizes the scope of work requirements, anticipated benefits, time schedule and expected consequences.

(ii) ***Ranking:*** Each decision package is ranked against packages for other proposed projects or activities and the projects that are running currently. Decision packages are ranked according to their benefits to the total organization during the budget period.

(iii) ***Resource allocation:*** Resources allocated to the packages according to the preferential rank in the organization. When properly executed the zero base budgeting provides an opportunity for the managers to carefully examine, evaluate and prioritize each organizational activity and see whether modification, continuance or termination is feasible.

Advantages of ZBB

(i) ZBB forces managers to critically examine the activities and projects to increase cost effectiveness.

(ii) It develops and promotes a professional cost reduction oriented spirit amongst the managers.

(iii) It places all the projects (existing as well as proposed) in competition.

(iv) It encourages grassroots participation in the process of budgeting.

Drawbacks of ZBB

(i) Excess paper work.

(ii) Time consuming process.

(iii) It is not suitable for big and growing organizations.

Application of ZBB

The heavy investment in time and the difficulties associated with ZBB suggest that it can be applied in small organizations, declining organizations and staff units of business firms.

FOR DISCUSSION

1. Define budgeting and budgetary control.
2. Discuss the purpose of budgeting in organization.
3. Discuss the types of budgets with suitable examples.
4. Discuss the budgeting process.
5. What is auditing?
6. Discuss the types of auditing.
7. What is computer aided planning and budgeting?
8. What are areas of computer aided planning?
9. Types of hardwares and softwares used for computer aided planning.
10. Define ZBB. How does it differ from normal budgeting?
11. Discuss the steps involved in ZBB.
12. Discuss the advantages and drawbacks of ZBB.

10

Human Resource Planning

Staffing is a very crucial function of management. For efficient functioning of the organization, competent incumbents are needed and staffing is the function, which provides human resource to the organization. The top line executives take ultimate decisions relating to staffing, the personnel department functions is the advisory and supporting capacity.

Definition

Staffing as the placement, growth and development of all those members of the organization whose functions is to get things done through the effort of other individuals. —*Theo Haimann*

Human Resource Planning

Human resource or Manpower refers to the knowledge, skills, creative abilities, talents and aptitudes of an organizations workforce as well as the individuals involved.

Human resource planning/Manpower planning may be defined as a strategy for the procurement, development, allocation and utilization of an enterprise's human resources. Procurement , of personnel deals with the task of recruitment and selection of workers of the desired skill mix. Training and development plans help in keeping and raising the skill standards of workers. Manpower allocation plans help in mitigating shortages and surpluses in manpower supply through promotions and transfers. Manpower utilization deals with dynamics of leadership and motivation.

Human resource planning or Manpower planning is the process by which a firm ensures that it has the right number of people and right kind of people and at the right places, at the right time and doing work for accomplishing objectives.

Objectives of Manpower Planning

(i) To ensure optimum use of human resources currently employed.

(ii) To determine future recruitment level.

(iii) To provide control measures to ensure that necessary resources are available as and when required.

(iv) To anticipate redundancies and avoid unnecessary dismissals.

(v) To forecast future skill requirements to serve as a basis for training and development programmes.

(vi) To assess future housing needs of employees.

(vii) To cost the manpower component in new projects.

(viii) To decide whether any of the enterprise's activities, e.g. maintenance be offloaded or sub-contracted.

Steps in Human resource planning

(i) Determining the organizational objectives.

(ii) Determining the skills and expertise required to achieve the organizational objectives.

(iii) Determining the additional human resource requirements based on the organizations current human resources.

(iv) Developing action plans to meet the anticipated human resource needs.

Planning Personnel Requirements

As both quantity and quality of workforce are important, personnel planning should be complete and detailed, but flexible and updated at least half yearly.

Recruitment

Once the requirement of manpower is known, the process of recruitment starts. It is defined as the process of identifying the source, prospective candidates and to stimulate them to apply for the jobs. In other words, recruitment is the generating of applications or applicants for specific positions.

The management should have a proper plan of recruitment regarding the quantity and quality of personnel required and the time when it is needed.

Sources of Recruitment

The source of recruitment can be classified into two categories *i.e.* internal and external. Internal sources refer to the present working force of a company. Vacancies other than at the lowest level may be filled by selecting individuals from amongst the existing employees of the company. The commonly used external, sources are the following:

External sources

(i) Reemploying former employees.
(ii) Friends and relatives of present employees.
(iii) Applicants at the gate.
(iv) College and technical institutions.
(v) Employment exchanges.
(vi) Advertising the vacancy.
(vii) Labour unions.

Selection

Manpower compares the qualifications of candidates with the requirements for a job and eliminates all those who do not stand up to this comparison. When the employees are placed in the job, which is suited for them, they derive maximum satisfaction and get more salary. Their overall efficiency will increase.

To determine the qualifications needed to meet the requirements of jobs, the company has first of all to analyze the job, job descriptions and prepare job specifications.

Job analysis: Determination of relevant information relating to the nature of job.

Job Description	Job Specification
A written description of a job and its requirements	A written statement of the necessary qualifications of the job incumbent
Job title and location	Education
Organizational-relationship	Experience
Relation to other jobs	Training exposure
Machine and materials	Mental abilities
Working conditions	Decision making
	Judgment

Placement

The process of placing the right man on the right job is called placement. It is an important aspect of selection process. A worker should be placed on a position where there is full use of the strengths and all his weaknesses become irrelevant. A misplaced person is always a frustrated individual.

Training

After selection of people for various jobs the next function of management is to arrange for their training and development. Training is important for new recruits and also for existing employees because of complications of new production techniques. Training is the act of increasing knowledge and skill of an employee for doing a particular job.

Forecasting

Forecasting is predicting beforehand the events, which may occur in the future and may greatly influence the functioning of the enterprise.

1. Demand Forecast: Stems from the objectives of the organization as represented in the company's plan. Hence to be able to forecast manpower demand in the future, the manpower planner must have a detailed knowledge of the company's future achievement targets. It is on the assumption of a given target level that this forecast is made.

Steps

(i) ***Selection of an Appropriate Basis for the Calculation of Manpower Needs:*** The basis must satisfy one important requirement—the required manpower be proportional to the changes in the basis, e.g. in a fertilizer manufacturing company, tons of fertilizer will serve as a useful basis for the calculation of manpower needs if the number of workers is proportional to the output of fertilizer.

(ii) ***Calculation of the Productivity Ratio:*** Output per individual is calculated for forecasting the number of men needed to carry out planned volume of work.

(iii) ***Making Adjustment in the Productivity Ratio:*** Making adjustment in the productivity ratio for likely improvements in it resulting from planned advances in technology, changes in organizational structure, training and better utilization of human resources.

(iv) ***Projection of Manpower Requirements:*** Organization can proceed to find out the ratios between the number of operatives and managerial personnel at various levels on the basis of certain assumptions about span of control, nature of work, technology and historical data.

Finally, with the help of these ratios it can work out the projections for its managerial personnel.

2. Supply Forecast

(i) ***Internal Supply Forecast:*** This is based on a study of the existing manpower resources and the potential losses and changes in them due to internal promotions, transfer, etc.

Probabilistic model—Markov Chain Analysis

Probabilities are calculated of the movement of people from one job to another in the organization or of leaving the organization on the basis of past record over some specified time period.

(ii) ***External Supply Forecast:*** The demand forecast and internal supply forecast match only in the most exceptional cases. In an expanding condition the supply will be less than demand. In a contrasting situation the supply will exceed the demand. In the expanding situation attention is generally given to increasing the supply by recruitment through other means to alter the supply (such as amendment in transfer and promotion policies, change in skill mix, etc. The following factors are considered for external forecasting:

(i) Population density at various distances from the work place.
(ii) Local employment level.
(iii) Availability of part-time labour.
(iv) Current competition for similar categories of labour from other organizations both local and national.
(v) Patterns of immigration and emigration within the area and other areas.
(vi) Local transport facilities and communication pattern.

Human Resource Information System (HRIS)

Maintaining systematic information about the individual employee: history, characteristics, performance record, potential record, promotions, other records, additional qualification, remarkable achievements, salaries, etc. This information also serves as a base for research on employee problems. Sometimes fresh data may be needed for identifying appropriate interventions for improving the utilization of human resources.

(i) Supply files to departments whenever solicited for counselling, career planning, training purposes.

(ii) Design data cards for computer.

(iii) Monitoring the data.

(iv) Process of data for research purpose, etc.

HR Audit

Study of existing manpower resources of the organization. Examining whether manpower strength for various jobs is inadequate or more than what should be employed. Collection of information like number of employees in each job and particulars about employees e.g. name, age, sex, educational qualification, skills, etc.

FOR DISCUSSION

1. Define HRP. What are the objectives of HRP?
2. Discuss the different steps involved in HRP with suitable examples.
3. What is forecasting?
4. Discuss Demand and Supply forecast and narrate the differences between them.
5. What is HRIS and HR Audit?

11

Motivation in Management

Motivation is an important factor, which encourages persons to give their best performance and help in reaching enterprise goals. A strong positive motivation will enable the increased output of employees but a negative motivation will reduce their performance.

Definition

A motive is an inner state that energizes, activates or moves and directs or channels behaviour towards goals. —*Berelson and Steiner*

Motivation refers to the degree of readiness of an organism to pursue some designated goal and implies the determination of the nature of the forces, including the degree of readiness. —*Encyclopedia of Management*

Motivation is the act of stimulating some one or oneself to get a desired course of action, to push the right button to get a desired reaction. —*Michael J. Julius*

Motivation can be defined as a willingness to expand energy to achieve a goal or a reward. —*Dale S. Beach*

Motivation is a predisposition to act in a specific goal directed way. —*S. Zedeck and H. Blood*

Characteristics of Motivation

(i) Motivation is a psychological phenomenon.

(ii) It is an internal feeling.

(iii) Motivation is dynamic and situational.

(iv) Motivation is not an easily observed phenomenon.

(v) It is a goal-oriented process.
(vi) It can be either positive or negative.
(vii) It is influenced by social and cultural norms.

Importance of Motivation

(i) ***Good Human Relations:*** A high level of motivation results in harmonious relations between employer and employees.

(ii) ***Low Absenteeism and Turnover:*** Motivation leads to job satisfaction and high morale due to which labour unrest, labour absenteeism and turnover are reduced.

(iii) ***Good Corporate Image:*** A company that provides adequate opportunities to its employees for the satisfaction of physical and psychological needs has a better image in the public.

(iv) ***Higher Efficiency:*** A good motivational system releases the immense talent and abilities of employees. It converts ability to work into will to work.

Process of Motivation

Unsatisfied need is the starting point in the process of motivation. It is the deficiency of something within the individual that provides the spark, which begins the chain of events leading to behaviour. An unsatisfied need causes tension (physical or psychological) within the individual to engage in some kind of behaviour to satisfy the need and thereby reduce the tension. This activity is directed towards a goal, arrival at goal satisfies the need and the process of motivation is complete.

Unsatisfied need
↓
Tension
↓
Drives
↓
Search behaviour
↓
Goal achievement
↓
Need satisfaction
↓
Reduction of tension

TECHNIQUES TO INCREASE MOTIVATION

Every employer tries that the persons working in his organization should be highly motivated. To achieve the organizational goals certain techniques to improve the employee morale are there but those techniques may not be similarly useful in all types of organizations.

(i) Non-financial motivators include recognition, participation, status, competition and job enrichment.

(ii) Financial motivators.

Non-financial Motivators

(i) *Recognition*: Every person wants that his work to be recognized by his superiors. When he knows that his superior knows his performance, he will try to improve it more and more. The recognition may be in the form of praise, a letter of appreciation and entry in actual confidential report, etc.

(ii) *Participation:* It implies physical and mental involvement of people in decision-making process. It satisfies ego and self esteem of persons. They feel important when asked to make suggestions in their field of activity.

(iii) *Status:* It refers to the social status of a person and it satisfies egoistic needs. A management may create some status symbols in the organization. This can be done by way of giving various facilities to the persons. These may be superior furniture, carpets on the floor, attachment of peons - personal assistant, etc.

(iv) *Competition:* In some organizations competition is used as a motivator. Various persons are given certain objectives and everybody tries to achieve them ahead of others. There may be praise, appreciation letters and financial incentives to those who reach the goals first. The competition encourages persons to improve their performance.

(v) *Job enrichment:* It has been recognized as an important motivator by various researchers. The job is made more important and challenging. An employee is given a free hand to decide and perform the work. It brings more job satisfaction and high morale.

Financial Motivators

It may be in the form of more wages and salaries, profit sharing, leave with pay, medical reimbursements, company paid insurance or any of the other things that may be given to employees for performance. Most managers consider money and financial incentives as important motivators.

Methods for Effective Motivation

Motivation is a very complex phenomenon. In order to motivate people towards organizational goals and effective actions, management has to create a congenial physical, social and psychological atmosphere. Human behaviour is influenced by a host of complex factors. Understanding these factors and adjusting them to suit the organizational need is essential for effective motivation. The following means can employ for effective employee motivation.

(i) ***Fair Remuneration:*** Most of the basic and many of the secondary human needs can be satisfied by fairly remunerating the employees. Nature of job, cost of living, pay scales of other organizations the wage structures and scales should properly be evaluated and determined.

(ii) ***Job Satisfaction:*** Management should place employees properly according to their merits, aptitudes, interests, and capacities. The well-placed employees take pride, interest and initiative in their work and derive job satisfaction.

(iii) ***Job Security:*** It is a great motivating factor. Security is a great psychological need of a map and hence must be satisfied for tuning up the morale.

(iv) ***Fair Promotions:*** Everybody aspires for growth and development in his life. Organizational promotions satisfy various physiological, social and psychological needs of the people. Management should arrange for promotional training and education to enable employees to get promotions. Promotions generate loyalty, hard working, discipline, initiative, courtesy, cooperation and overall hopes and aspirations in the behaviour of the employees.

(v) ***Congenial Working Environment:*** Working conditions for the employees must be made congenial. The adequate provision of light, air, safety, sanitation, cleanliness, noise prevention, smoke and fume clearance should be made for physical health and mental health and satisfaction. Congenial environment releases tension and tiredness and motivate them to work.

(vi) ***Honest and Competent Leadership:*** If the leaders and managers are honest, impartial, sympathetic and capable of understanding employee hopes and aspirations, emotions and sentiments, prospects and problems, motives and attitudes they would be able to win the control, maintain discipline and motivate their employees.

(vii) ***Efficient Organization, Coordination and Control:*** Efficient organization may include adequate and efficient physical facilities and organization of manpower. Proper delegation of authority and fixation of responsibilities avoid confusion and conflicts to bring unity in action and purpose. To the great extent the feeling of security, certainty, fairness, confidence, interest and initiative is a result of efficient organization, coordination and control.

(viii) ***Efficient System of Grievance Redressal:*** Employee grievance is a major factor detracting employees from work and forming an apathetic attitude towards management. If management introduces a perfect system of discovering the employee grievances, their causes and remedies and remove them honestly and regularly, it will win the confidence of the employees.

(ix) ***Freedom of Association, Mobility Expression etc.:*** The need of association or of gregariousness is a great need of human beings. Management should satisfy this need by providing freedom to individuals from their cultural and social association whether formal or informal.

(x) ***Democratic Management Techniques:*** If the employees are given participation in management decisions, they begin to feel themselves as a part and parcel of the organization. It satisfies their instinct of belonging to the organization, gives them psychological satisfaction and fosters the feeling of team and cooperation.

(xi) ***Other Incentives:*** Several other physical and psychological incentives may be offered by the management to tune up employee morale and motivate them towards stated objectives. The efficient training programmes, the affectionate attitude of superiors towards their subordinates and such innumerable measures can motivate people.

Motivation Theories

1. Abraham H. Maslow's Need Hierarchy Model
2. Alderfer's ERG Model
3. Herzberg's Two-factor Theory
4. Maturity-Immaturity Theory
5. Mc Clelland's Achievement Motivation Theory
6. J. Stacy Adam's Equity Theory
7. Vroom's expectancy theory
8. McGregor's Theory X and Y

1. Abraham H. Maslow's need hierarchy model: He proposed that basic needs are structured in a hierarchy of prepotency and probability of appearance. He considered several needs to; explain human behaviour and proposed that these needs have a hierarchy that some needs are lower order needs as compared to others. Unless the need at the lower level is satisfied, the higher order need will not be operative and once the lower order need is satisfied it will no more motivate the person. He proposed five main hierarchical levels in the needs.

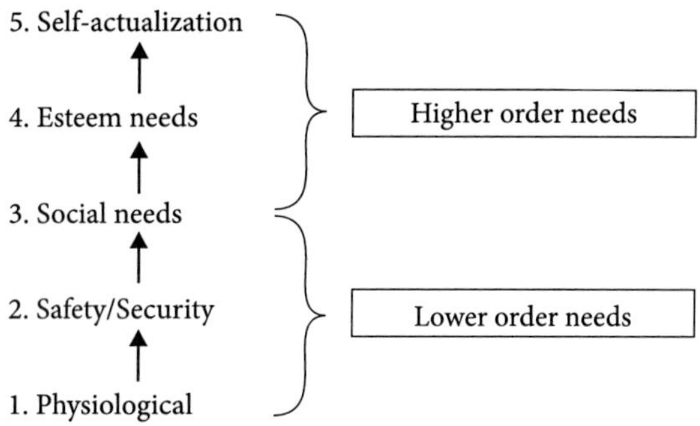

(i) *Physiological needs:* These are the biological needs required to preserve human life and it include need for food, thirst, shelter and sex. These needs will dominate when all needs are unsatisfied.

(ii) *Safety needs:* Safety needs include protection from physical harm, ill health, economic disaster and avoidance of the unexpected.

(iii) *Social needs:* They are related to the social nature of people and their needs for companionship. Non-satisfaction of this level may affect the mental health of the individual.

(iv) *Esteem needs:* These needs consist both of the need for awareness of importance to others and the actual esteem by others. Satisfaction of these needs leads to a feeling of self confidence and prestige.

(v) *Self-actualization needs:* Desire to become more and more what one is to become, everything one is capable of becoming. This means that individual will fully realize the potentialities of talents and capabilities.

2. Alderfer's ERG Model: Clayton Alderfer's modified need hierarchy model into three: Existence, Relatedness and Growth (ERG)

(i) *Existence (Physiological needs and Safety needs):* Needs required to preserve human life. They include all of what Maslow termed as Basic needs and safety needs.

(ii) *Relatedness (Social):* They refer to all socially intended needs *i.e.* how people relate to their surrounding environment. These include the need for meaningful social and interpersonal relationship.

(iii) *Growth (Esteem and Self actualization):* They reflect the individuals desire to be self confident, productive and creative, the desire to engage in tasks that requires the full utilization of abilities and that develop additional capabilities/skills.

3. Herzberg's two-factor Theory: Frederick Herzberg provided an interesting extension of Maslow's need hierarchy theory and developed a specific content theory of work motivation. It is also called the dual factor theory and the motivation-hygiene theory of motivation.

(i) *Hygiene factor:* When absent, increase dissatisfaction with the job and when present, do not increase satisfaction.

(ii) *Motivation factor:* When absent, prevent both satisfaction and motivation. When present, lead to satisfaction and motivation.

S. No.	Hygiene/Maintenance /Extrinsic	Motivators/Satisfier /Intrinsic
1.	Company policy & administration	1. Achievement
2.	Relationship with supervisors	2. Recognition
3.	Work situation	3. Work itself
4.	Salary	4. Responsibility
5.	Relationship with peers	5. Advancement
6.	Personal life	6. Growth
7.	Relationship with subordinates	
8.	Status	
9.	Security	
10.	Supervision	

4. Maturity-Immaturity Theory: Chris Argyris has postulated a descriptive and multidimensional developmental process along which individuals in an organization grow. He examined industrial organizations to determine the effect of management practices an individual behaviour and their personal growth within work environment. He noticed seven basic changes that take place in the mature people over the years.

According to him people in work Organizations will have a tendency to grow from an infant to a matured state. The mature state is characterized by an endless series of challenges in which the reward Comes from doing something for its own sake. The matured employee is characterized by full blown, wholeness, complexity and depth of knowledge and behaves like an adult.

Immaturity	**Maturity**
Passive	Active
Dependence	Independence
Behave in a few ways	Capable of behaving in a variety of ways
Shallow abilities	Developing few abilities in depth
Having a short time perspective	Long term perspective
Subordinate position	Subordinate or equal position
Lack of self-awareness	Awareness and control over self

5. Mc Clelland's Achievement Motivation Theory: David Mc Clelland (1950) studied three needs that motivate human behaviour—*power, affiliation and achievement.* He believes that each person has a need for all three (as well as for others) but that people differ in the degree to which the various needs motivate their behaviour.

(i) *Power:* The employee exhibiting the need for power derives satisfaction from the ability to control other organizations such as the military and Government that foster the power motivate tend to attract people with a high need for power.

(ii) *Affiliation:* Employees with a high need for affiliation derive satisfaction from social and interpersonal activities.

(iii) *Achievement:* Employees with a high need for an achievement derive satisfaction from reaching goals. High achievers prefer immediate feedback as their performance, and they generally undertake tasks of moderate difficulty rather than those that are either very easy or very difficult.

6. J. Stacy Adam's Equity Theory: This theory pointed out that people are motivated to maintain fair relationships with others and will try to rectify unfair relationships by making them fair. It is based on two assumptions

(i) Individuals make contributions (inputs) for which they expect certain outcomes (rewards). Inputs include such things as person's training and experience, special knowledge, personal characteristics, etc. Outcomes include pay, recognition, promotion, prestige, fringe benefits, etc.

(ii) Individuals decide whether or not a particular exchange is satisfactory by comparing their inputs and outcomes to those of others in the form of a ratio.

(a) Overpayment Equity: Person gets more out of the job relatively to what he puts in compared to others

$$\frac{\text{Person's outcomes}}{\text{Person's inputs}} > \frac{\text{Other's outcomes}}{\text{Others input}}$$

(b) Equity: $$\frac{\text{Person's outcomes}}{\text{Person's inputs}} = \frac{\text{Other's outcomes}}{\text{Others input}}$$

In this situation both x and y obtain the same relative gain for their investments

(c) Underpayment Equity

$$\frac{\text{Person's outcomes}}{\text{Person's inputs}} < \frac{\text{Other's outcomes}}{\text{Others input}}$$

In this situation the person and the other do the same job but other gets paid more and the person experiences dissonance.

7. Vroom's Expectancy Theory: Victor Vroom presented the expectancy theory (1964) as an alternative to conventional theories. The motivational relationship may be expressed in the form of a formula

Motivation = V × E × I (Valence, Expectancy, Instrumentality)

(i) *Valence* (*Preferences*)**:** Strength of an individual's desire for a particular outcome. Refers to the personal value workers place on the rewards they believe they will receive for performing.

(ii) *Expectancy:* Refers to the extent to which the person believes that his efforts will lead to the first level outcome *i.e.* Performance.

(iii) *Instrumentality:* Relationship between performance and rewards. It provides answer to such question: Will I be rewarded if I perform the job well?

8. Theory X and Theory Y: Mc Gregor believed that the manager normally attempts to motivate employees by one of the two basic approaches:

(i) Theory X—Organization is controlled and directed through the exercise of authority. Autocratic style, one-way communication, non-participation, centralized control and supervision.

(ii) Theory Y—Democratic style, two-way communication, Active participation, decentralized control and supervision.

Role of Manager in the Context of Internal and External Environment

Manager is a planner, producer, marketer and is the man who is expected to make things happen. He is the pivotal figure and the primary instrument in the technical task of the creation of wealth. Every organization exists within a highly complex environment that exerts a dominant influence on its composition and operation. To obtain optimum level of performance in his organization, the manager must have a clear understanding of these forces within his environment, the nature and importance of his interaction with them.

Manager's dual personality as that of an employee in the case of internal environment and that of a citizen in the case of external environment.

1. Internal Environment—Manager as an Employee

In the internal environment the important roles of managers are that of the following:

(i) Leadership
(ii) Coordinating
(iii) Decision-making
(iv) Delegator of authority
(v) A symbol of authority
(vi) A standard setter in business
(vii) Human relations practitioner
(viii) Public relations man
(ix) A creator of order
(x) A trustee

2. External Environment: As a Negotiator and a Spokesperson

In the external environment the managers should have good relationship with the following:

1. Economic relations
   Capital-Investors and creditors
   Labour
   Suppliers
   Customers and consumers
2. Technological relations
3. Social-community relations
4. Political relations
5. Ethical/Principles

FOR DISCUSSION

1. Define motivation and process of motivation.
2. Explain the importance of motivation in an organization.
3. What are the techniques for increasing motivation of employees?
4. Explain the different methods for effective motivation of employees in an organization.
5. Discuss different theories of motivation with suitable examples.
6. Explain the role of manager in internal and external environment.

12

Organizationl Communication and Management Information System

Communication is a natural instinct of all living creatures. It is the basic need of all human beings. It plays all the more significant role in the present day organizations which are complex, dynamic and socially oriented. Effective communication keeps the organization vibrant, vital and smooth sailing.

The word communication has been derived from the latin word 'communis' which means common. It involves transmission of some information by one person to another who receives and understands it in the same sense.

Definition

The communication pattern existing in a Government office, business organisation, etc., which is duly controlled by the members of those organisations and it is intended only to the members. It is also called as Administrative Communication.

Importance of Organizational Communication

(i) Basis of decision-making
(ii) Facilitates coordination
(iii) Sound industrial relations
(iv) Smooth and efficient operations
(v) Industrial democracy
(vi) Employee motivation and morale
(vii) Public relations

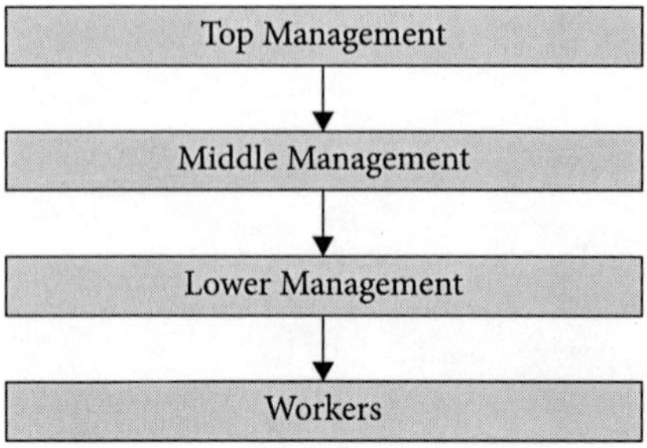

TYPES OF ORGANIZATIONAL COMMUNICATION

Downward Communication

It is also referred to as superior-subordinate communication. The source is located at a higher level in the organization design than the information receiver. The purpose of downward communication is to give information, orders, and instructions to subordinate or to solicit information from them.

Barriers in Downward Communication

(i) Badly expressed ideas
(ii) Faulty translations
(iii) Distrust of the superior
(iv) Lack of confidence in subordinates
(v) Lack of communication skill and ability
(vi) Inattention of the subordinate
(vii) Difference in experience and background
(viii) Physical barriers—environmental factors
(ix) Body language

Upward Communication

It is also referred to as subordinate-superior communication. It takes place in the form of progress reports, complaints grievances, opinion, attitudes, suggestions, etc. Thus, the purpose of upward communication is to provide a channel for funneling information, opinion and attitudes up through the organization.

Barriers in Upward Communication

(i) Concealment of the feelings by the subordinates
(ii) Belief that management is not interested in employee problems

(iii) Difference in experience and background
(iv) Stereotypes and beliefs
(v) Status differentials
(vi) Language problem
(vii) Filtering
(viii) Incorrect timing

Downward communication and upward communication are also called as Interscalar Communication. It is the communication between personnel at different levels in the hierarchy.

Horizontal Communication

It is also referred to as lateral communication and it takes place among the work groups at the same organizational level. There is no authority flowing along the line of horizontal communication.

Thus the purpose of horizontal communication is to assure work coordination and to provide psychological and social support for the organization members.

Formal Communication

Communication through the chain of command is known as formal communication. It is planned and established by management. It indicates clearly the authority relationships involved. It involves the transmission of official messages, or information in the formal organization structure. It may be oral or written/vertical or horizontal. The principle of 'single line of command' is followed in a formal communication.

Informal Communication

Communication arising out of the informal relations is known as informal communication or the grapevine. It is not established by the management. It does not flow through the formal or official channel of communication. It involves the spontaneous expression of ideas and reactions. It is built around the social relationship of the members of an organization. It arises out of the social interaction of the people.

Informal communication is implicit, spontaneous and flexible while formal communication is explicit, articulate, rigid and direct.

Channels of Informal Communication

- Grapevine is a channel for rumour and gossip, canteen lunch and social occasions.

Grapevine Communication

It arises from social interaction. Typical situations in which *Grapevine Communication* is very active are as follows:

Excitement and insecurity

Involvement of friends and associates

Recent information

Procedure that brings people into contact

Work that allows conversation

Job that provides information decided by others

Personality of communicator

Ways to Improve Communication

The following are the some of ways for improving communication:

1. Visual Cues

- Facial expression
- Eye contact
- Body positioning
- Hand gestures
- Style of dress
- Physical appearance
- Body movements

2. Vocal Cues

Vocal cues include regional dialects, methods of pronunciation and the five major factors:

(i) Volume—speaking with adequate loudness is the first responsibility of any communicator.

(ii) Rate and fluency—if the person is able to articulate well, a faster rate seems to be more interesting to listen to.

(iii) Pitch—refers to the frequency in cycles per second (CPS) of the vocal tones.

(iv) Quality—refers to the resonance of the voice.

(v) Inflection—refers to the relative emphasis, pitch changes, and duration in uttering different word parts in a sentence.

Improving listening skills: When we can make the other person feel really understood, we are often seen as effective communicators.

(i) Pay attention and show positive non-verbal behaviour.
(ii) Listen for content. Describe what you hear, then attempt to state what it means to you.
(iii) Try not to interrupt.
(iv) Try not to argue mentally.
(v) Ask for clarification rather than assuming you know what is meant.
(vi) Avoid side conversations.

Practical Tips on How to Communicate Effectively in a Team Setting

(i) Express your own ideas clearly and logically, but avoid arguing blindly for them. Consider other viewpoints.
(ii) Change your mind based on the logical points of others. Do not change your mind only to avoid conflict.
(iii) See a consensus decision.
(iv) Encourage people to become involved and speak their minds.
(v) Discuss underlying assumptions and ideas.
(vi) Strive for a win-win solution that incorporates the best of all ideas.
(vii) Reconsider an earlier decision.

Management Information System (MIS)

MIS is an integrated technique for gathering relevant information from whatever source it originates and transferring it into usable form for the decision makers in management. It is a system of communication primarily designed to keep all levels of organizational personnel abreast of the developments in the enterprise that affect them. MIS provides working tools for all management personnel in order to take the best possible action at the right time with respect to the operations and functions of the enterprise for which they are largely responsible.

Definition

Management information system is defined as a formal system of gathering, integrating, comparing, analyzing and dispersing information internal and external to the enterprise in a timely, effective and efficient manner.

Need for MIS

MIS stresses the information that is most useful, not just pieces of paper. MIS undertakes collection of all forms and regular charts and reports and then subjects them to a series of interpretation, refinement and consolidation. It reduces the burden of the chief executive and the departmental head, personnel who are overloaded with the facts.

It should be noted that all MIS systems are computer based. Smaller organizations may use MIS by manual system. However, large organizations typically use computers in conjunction with software that give directions to the computer what to do. Computer has an impressive capability for analyzing huge quantities of data in a more accurate fashion and removes any perceived complexities in interpretation of data.

Three-prolonged Service

MIS performs a useful triple service function to management. Actually, MIS is a three-phase process:

(i) Data generation
(ii) Data processing
(iii) Information transmission

Collection of data in the case of a large organization is not an easy task. An effective management information system systematically and accurately collects the required information from various departments. Secondly, the major task of processing the data is undertaken by MIS to produce the output information.

MIS provides answers to all these critical questions. MIS, thus objectively determines with a minimum controversy what information is needed by whom and with what frequency.

Application and Impacts of Computers

The personal computer is becoming increasingly appealing to managers because it is flexible and relatively inexpensive and can be used more quickly than the mainframe computer. Its application includes the following:

(i) Budget preparation
(ii) Graphic presentation
(iii) Electronic spread sheets
(iv) Financial analysis
(v) Word processing

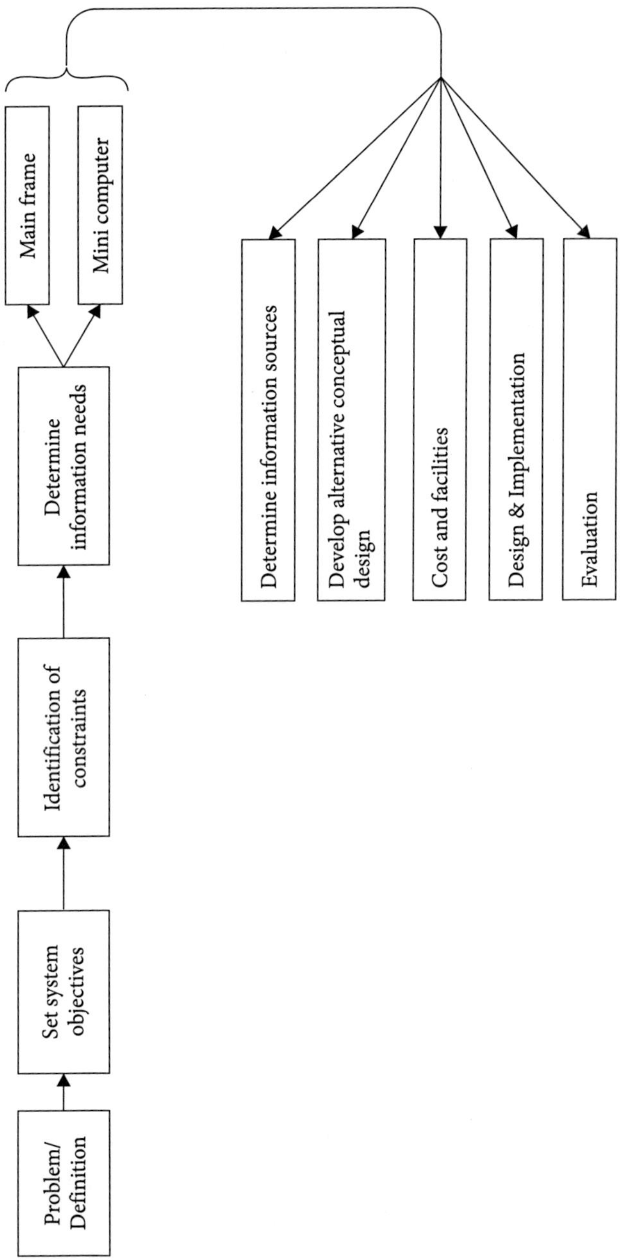
Problem/ Definition
Set system objectives
Identification of constraints
Determine information needs
Main frame
Mini computer
Determine information sources
Develop alternative conceptual design
Cost and facilities
Design & Implementation
Evaluation

(vi) Simulation models

(vii) Forecasting

(viii) E-mail

(ix) Data bases

Information Technology

Due to the recent revolution in information technology access to information across the globe has become very quick and cost-effective.

Speech Recognition Devices

Another way to encourage the use of computer is through speech recognition devices. There are many complex problems involved in developing speech recognition devices, but the efforts made in this area result in products that may revolutionize office operation.

Telecommunicating

The widespread use of computer and the ease linking them through telephone line to a company's mainframe computer has led to telecommunicating. This means that a person can work at a computer terminal at home instead of commuting to work place.

Computer Networks

Computer networks have been developed with link workstations. Persons at several workstations can communicate with each other as well as access other computers. There are many other applications of computer networks, such as e-mail and disseminating industry data and future trends.

Advantages of MIS

(i) MIS performs triple service functions:

Data generation

Data processing

Information transmission

(ii) It enhances the management's ability to plan, measure and control performance and taking necessary corrective action.

(iii) It facilitates total performance:

Provides technical and special kind of information

Multiple type of information for all management levels

(iv) MIS takes into account the most important dimensions such as:

Real time requirement (how timely the information should be)

Frequency requirement (how often the information must be available or furnished)

Accuracy requirement (how detailed or correct the information must be)

Data reduction requirement (where the information must be supplied)

Storage requirement (where the information must be stored)

(v) It reduces overload of information and it stresses the information that is most useful to the decision maker.

(vi) An effective implementation of MIS is likely to result in substantial benefits by providing managers with the necessary information for planning, decision-making, performance, performance evaluation, coordination and control.

FOR DISCUSSION

1. Define organizational communication.
2. Discuss downward, upward, formal and informal communication with examples.
3. What is grapevine communication? What are the sources of grapevine communication?
4. What are the ways for improving communication?
5. Define MIS. Discuss the need of MIS in organization
6. Discuss the steps in MIS and application of IT in MIS.
7. Advantages of MIS in organization.

13

Tools of Network Analysis

Network Analysis

A network is a set of symbols connected with each other with a sequential relationship with each step making the completion of a project/event. There is a need for deciding the sequential order of all activities of the project so as to accomplish the project economically in the minimum available time with limited resources. Some of the tools used for network analysis are PERT, CPM, etc.

Programme Evaluation and Review Technique (PERT)

It was introduced in 1950 and developed jointly by the navy special projects office and Booz Allen Hamilton in conjunction with the fleet ballistic missile programme with the objective to reduce the time span for the Polaris Ballistic Missile project of U.S. Navy.

It is an invaluable aid to the planning and controlling of major and complex projects particularly to analyze and control the timing aspects of these projects.

Definition

It is a sophisticated, mathematical and schematic network technique use for planning and control.

Elements of PERT

(i) Activity: Represented by arrow.

(ii) Events: Represented by circles.

(iii) Path: The network connecting a series of activities and events.

A programme, which consists of several activities that should be completed in a proper sequence and in allotted time. For this purpose, a network is developed to show the sequence, time of start, and time of end of particular activities. The whole process is a function of PERT/CPM.

Steps Involved in the Preparation of PERT

(i) Identification of activities.

(ii) Sequential arrangements of activities.

(iii) Time estimates of activities.

(iv) Network construction.

(v) Preparation of critical path.

PERT programme has three time estimates:

(i) *Optimistic Time:* An estimate of the time required to complete the project if everything goes exceptionally well

(ii) *Must Likely Time:* How much time required to complete the project under normal circumstances

(iii) *Pessimistic Time:* Given the worst conditions, what is the time taken for completion of the project

These estimates are averaged giving special weightage to most likely estimates and a single estimate is used for calculations

$$t_e = \frac{O_t + 4M + P_t}{6}$$

Advantages of PERT

(i) It determines the expected time required for completing each activity.

(ii) It helps complete the project within a given period of time.

(iii) It helps management handle uncertainties involved in the project and thus reduce the risk elements in the project.

(iv) It enables management to make optimum allocation of limited resources.

(v) It presses for the right action at the right point and at the right time in the organization.

Critical Path Method (CPM)

It was first developed in USA by the E.I. Dupont Nemours and Co. in 1956 for doing periodic overhauling and maintenance of a chemical plant. It resulted in reducing the shut down period from 130 hrs to 90 hrs and saving the company $ 1 million. It is a commonly used term for all network analysis and aid for planning and controlling complicated projects. It refers to the sequence of events which takes the longest time and which has minimum or zero stack time. It is the longest path from the beginning of the event to the end event. CPM is found both for normal time, normal cost and for crash time and crash cost in case of early completion of project. The duration of the different activities in CPM are deterministic. There is a precise known time that each activity in the project will take.

Advantages of CPM

(i) It helps in ascertaining the time schedule of activities having sequential relationship.

(ii) It makes control easier for the management.

Difference between PERT and CPM

S.No	PERT	CPM
1.	Its origin is Military	Its origin is Industry
2.	It is an event oriented approach	It is an activity oriented approach
3.	It allows uncertainty	It does not allow uncertainty
4.	It is applied for planning and scheduling research	Used for construction and business problems
5.	It is a probabilistic model	Deterministic model
6.	It emphasizes only time	It deals with time as well as costs associated. It introduces a concept of critical path
7.	It operates three time estimates (Optimum, Most likely, Pessimistic)	Provides two estimates Normal time, Normal cost and Crash time and Crash cost (Trade off between cost and time)
8	It is suitable when high precision is required in time estimates *e.g.* Defense projects	It is suitable when reasonable precision is required, *e.g.* Civil, construction projects, Industrial expansion schemes, etc.

(iii) It identifies the most critical elements in the project. Thus, the management is kept alert and prepared to pay due attention to the critical activities of the project.

(iv) It makes better and detailed planning possible.

PERT and CPM make use of flow diagrams or network made up of a series of related events and activities for planning, scheduling, controlling and progress on a given programme. Events are most frequently represented by circle or square symbols. Activities being the time consuming factor of the programme are used to connect the various events.

FOR DISCUSSION

1. Define Network analysis.
2. What is PERT? Explain the elements of PERT.
3. Define CPM. Discuss the advantages of CPM.
4. Differentiate between PERT and CPM.

14

Management by Objectives (MBO)

In the present changing economic environment old techniques of management do not give better results. The expansion of business and changes in technology has necessitated a new thinking in managerial approach. A number of new techniques of management have been developed in the recent past and management by objectives (MBO) is one of them. Peter Drucker, a noted management writer introduced the term MBO in 1954. MBO is also known by the names management by motivation, management by exception, management by results, etc.

Definition

MBO is a dynamic system, which seeks to integrate the company's needs to clarify and achieve its profit and growth goals with the manager's need to contribute and develop himself. It is a demanding and rewarding style of managing a business. —*J. W. Humble*

MBO is a comprehensive managerial system that integrates many key managerial activities in a systematic manner, consciously directed towards the effective and efficient achievement of organizational objectives. —*Koontz and O' Donnell*

MBO is a process whereby superior and subordinate managers of an organization jointly define its common goals, define each individual's major areas of responsibility in terms of results expected of him and use these measures as guides for operating the unit and assessing the contribution of each of its members. —*Odiorne*

Features of MBO

(i) MBO focuses on goals and their achievement.

(ii) MBO tries to relate the long term goals of the organization with the short range goals, overall system goals with the goals of various sub-systems and the organizational goals.

(iii) MBO recognizes the fact that the goal setting and achievement process is a cooperative and participation endeavour.

(iv) MBO places emphasis not merely on goals, but on effective performance and tangible results also.

(v) MBO aims at a radical realignment of relations between superior and subordinate managers. Superior managers are required to adopt a supportive simulative role in relation to their subordinates.

(vi) The technique of MBO establishes a community of interest and a shared vision amongst all the managers.

PROCEDURES/STEPS INVOLVED IN MBO

1. Specifying Objectives: Objectives should include the three types of interrelated objectives namely: (a) purpose of an organization, (b) strategic and long term objective and (c) short-term objectives. Objectives both for the organization and its units are essential, as otherwise individual manager's contribution cannot be identified within the area of his operation.

2. Setting Objectives: Setting objectives is as important as the output (results). The objective should be specific, clear and without any ambiguity. They should be attainable, *i.e.* within the reach of the person concerned. They should be stimulating, motivating and challenging. Maintenance of hierarchy in setting objectives is important, *i.e.* before lower level objectives can be set, it is necessary that specific and clear top management objectives must be set and then further on such objectives should be set throughout the organization.

3. Reviewing and Validating Objectives: Research in MBO and behavioural sciences suggest that any programme works better if its performance is reviewed and objectives validated, regularly through feedback not necessarily after a year but profitably quarterly and even monthly.

4. Implementing Objectives: While implementing the objectives it is essential to have a correct assessment of the present position in respect of management rules, procedures, systems, managers attitudes and external environment. Organization structure and past performance of an organization are very much linked with the implementation strategy. Implementation requires commitment, sincerity of purpose, hard work, good understanding, time effect, patience and planning.

5. Controlling and Evaluating Objectives: This is the final step in the process of MBO. It is concerned with the evaluation and review of objectives. Here objectives are matched against performance. If there are any errors detected, corrective action is taken and guidance on future achievements is provided. MBO tends to emphasize quantitative rather than qualitative aspects of performance in terms of goals and achievements.

Advantages/Benefits of MBO

(a) Benefits for the Enterprise

(i) MBO lays great emphasis on the development and utilization of human resources.

(ii) It facilitates the enterprise ability to organizational change.

(iii) Problem areas of management including structures, strategies and practices are well identified by MBO.

(iv) It renders planning more specific and purposeful.

(v) It helps in clarifications to the objectives and focuses managers' efforts towards their achievement.

(vi) It helps bringing coordination and cooperation in the enterprise efforts by highlighting interdependence and improving communication.

(vii) It helps in managing centralized operations, laying emphasis on delegation of authority.

(viii) MBO is applicable to any part of the organization.

(ix) MBO being flexible in nature, degree of its implementation can be made use in any manner for achievement of organizational objectives.

(x) Voluntary commitments for performance by the employees in an organization come forth as a result of MBO involvement.

(b) Benefits for Superiors

(i) MBO provides participative atmosphere, helps the superior in coaching the subordinates.

(ii) MBO stimulates motivating subordinates to give better performance by committing themselves to achieve a set of results agreed through participation.

(c) Benefits for Employees

(i) It enhances employee job satisfaction.

(ii) While setting goals for individuals it makes clear what is expected of the employees.

(iii) It provides measurable objectives that the employee is expected to achieve.

Problems with MBO

(i) ***Distrust in MBO Ideology:*** MBO has come forth as a new approach and way of thinking about management. Some of the middle and lower level managers who are used to traditional authoritarian thinking, outlook and way of doing things, feel suspicious about top executive thinking and action in terms of MBO. They take it as a clever move on the part of the management to extract harder work from them under the cloak of MBO.

(ii) ***Time Consuming:*** MBO is very time consuming in the short run. Since it involves two-way communication, which necessitates discussions, exchange of Views between superior and subordinates, so there is increased pressure on time.

(iii) ***Resistance to Paper Work:*** There is so much writing work generated refilling of various forms, etc., and proposals, reviewing and reporting, which pose a problem to MBO in its smooth working.

(iv) ***Interruptions:*** In the case of public sector undertakings there is much frequent shifting of top-level managers who are most concerned with the working of MBO system in the undertaking. With this shifting the system gets interrupted, shows slackness and no wonder in some cases it may virtually come to a stop.

(v) ***Unwanted Forced Acceptance of the System :*** It is bound to strike in the minds of the subordinates that this system has been forced on them. They will naturally take it very disinterestedly, with the result, it will not work towards achieving the objectives.

(vi) ***Despondency and Despair:*** When top managers simply watch the things happen, the changes as expected does not come soon because of internal, external and other factors. Such a situation naturally brings a state of despondency and despair to prevail in the minds of lower level managers.

(vii) ***Information Constraints and Compulsions:*** In some cases difficulties are experienced in making available historical and other data and experience, pertinent to the investigation and analysis.

(viii) ***Limits in Measuring Objectives:*** MBO is not an all means for measuring performance. There may be some objectives and goals within reach of measurement by MBO.

LIMITATIONS IN MBO

(i) The Puzzling Details: The details like what gains to the enterprise, to the superiors and subordinates it ultimately holds, remain all a puzzle to the managers who have to practise it. Managers need to study all this thoroughly and have a clear understanding of the various activities connected with its application and working.

(ii) Lack of Direction and Guidance to Goal Setters: Goal setting forms the very nucleus of MBO. For any lack or insufficiency of direction and guidance to the personnel who are supposed to involve themselves in goal setting, no MBO plans can work.

- **(a)** ***Problems in Goal Setting:*** Setting realistic and true goals always remain a problem particularly when they have a pinch of time period; say quarterly, half yearly or yearly.
- **(b)** ***Snag in Short-term goals:*** The short run goals may not sometimes prove to be efficient in achieving the objectives.

(iii) Hazardous inflexibility: Managers hesitate to bring about any change in objectives and they remain stick up to objectives once determined for the period.

FOR DISCUSSION

1. Define MBO.
2. Discuss the principles of MBO.
3. Explain the steps involved in MBO.
4. Discuss the advantages of MBO in organization
5. Discuss the problems and limitations of MBO.

15

A Systematic Approach (ASA) and Innovative Extension Approaches

ASA is a systematic approach developed in UK in 1965 for giving training and consultancy services for the company. It came to India during 1977 and started collaboration with World Bank Project.

STEPS TO CARRY OUT ASA

1. Aims: Aims encompasses objectives, task, mission, ideas, etc. Three different aspects of aims like purpose, end result and success criterion.

Purpose: Why are we doing a particular task? What is it for? Who is it for? Clarify aims by deciding the future we want to create. What is to what ought to be?

e.g. We can use in order to What is it for—To increase yield.

Who is it for—For farmers.

End results: What we want to achieve after completion of the task?

Success criterion: Standards for evaluating performance to quantify end results.

How can we assess end product, to say confidently that it is what is required? If standards are achieved, results are obtained.

2. Getting Things done in Two Phases:

Information Stage: Collection of all relevant information that are already available. What more is required? Interpret and process information considering options and identifying risks involved.

Planning Stage: What has to be done and who will do it?

3. Action: Doing it according to planning.

4. Review: We are assessing results achieved with relation to aims, analyzing successes and difficulties so as to plan for improvement at individual level, team level, etc.

Advantages of ASA

(i) Through this approach thinking skill of an individual is improved. Strength of each individual is made use of.

(ii) It is directed at getting things done and drawing lessons from experiences.

(iii) It makes us more aware of stages of thought processes.

(iv) It enables to recover a logical sequence if we deviate from the plan.

(v) It provides framework to present our thoughts in a way that others can follow.

(vi) It provides common language for all people to follow.

(vii) It pinpoints the strengths and weaknesses of the activities.

Broad Based Extension System (BBES)

BBES has been introduced in Tamil Nadu State from 1.4.1991. Government of Tamil Nadu has entered into agreements with World Bank through Government of India for implementing the project.

Need for BBES

This system was formed to encourage the activities of the farmers. Different departments compete with one another and they have proposed to increase the staff component to contact as many farmers as possible. World Bank and GOI thought to utilize the well-established extension agency and bring all extension activities together.

Principles of BBES

(i) Adoption of integrated farming systems approach for the generation of relevant composite messages.

(ii) Broadening the range of subjects from agricultural crops to all allied subjects.

(iii) Improvement of the effective communication of the farming community.

(iv) Introduction of resource based planning down to sub-division level.

(v) Encourage participation of non-Governmental organizations in all agricultural extension activities.

Objectives of the BBES

(i) To increase the farm income.
(ii) To solve problems of the farming community.
(iii) To make extension system most cost effective.
(iv) To upgrade the quality of the extension workers.
(v) To popularize integrated farming system approach.

Scope of BBES

The activities of all land-based departments will be unified in the long run. Duplication of efforts and unhealthy competitions will be avoided. Agricultural department offers full support to the activities of all the line departments.

BBES helps the farmers in getting multiple message needed to improve their overall economy besides helping to grow agricultural activities, growing good fodders, animal husbandry activities and growing fish in the farm ponds, etc.

BBES involves the coordination of line departments with the agricultural department. Agricultural department will serve as nodal department, e.g., in NWDPRA area messages delivered will cover agricultural department, agricultural engineering and forest department for land treatment, vegetative bunding, selection of trees, etc. In hilly areas horticultural department will deliver messages.

It can be concluded that the BBES will help the farmer to obtain composite messages suitable to his agriculture as well as to his allied activities. The agricultural extension system will work in close coordination with line departments. The farmer is expected to derive maximum benefits from this system.

Satellite Model Farm Approach/Concept (SMFA)

With a view to accomplish the goals and objectives of the BBES in general and Tamil Nadu Agricultural Development Project (TNADP) in particular, the Tamil Nadu Agricultural University has developed a new strategy called Satellite Model Farm Approach (SMFA) based on the findings and field testing experiences of the ICAR sponsored action research project entitled 'An alternative Model for T&V system' proposed by the authors. The project was implemented for a period of two years

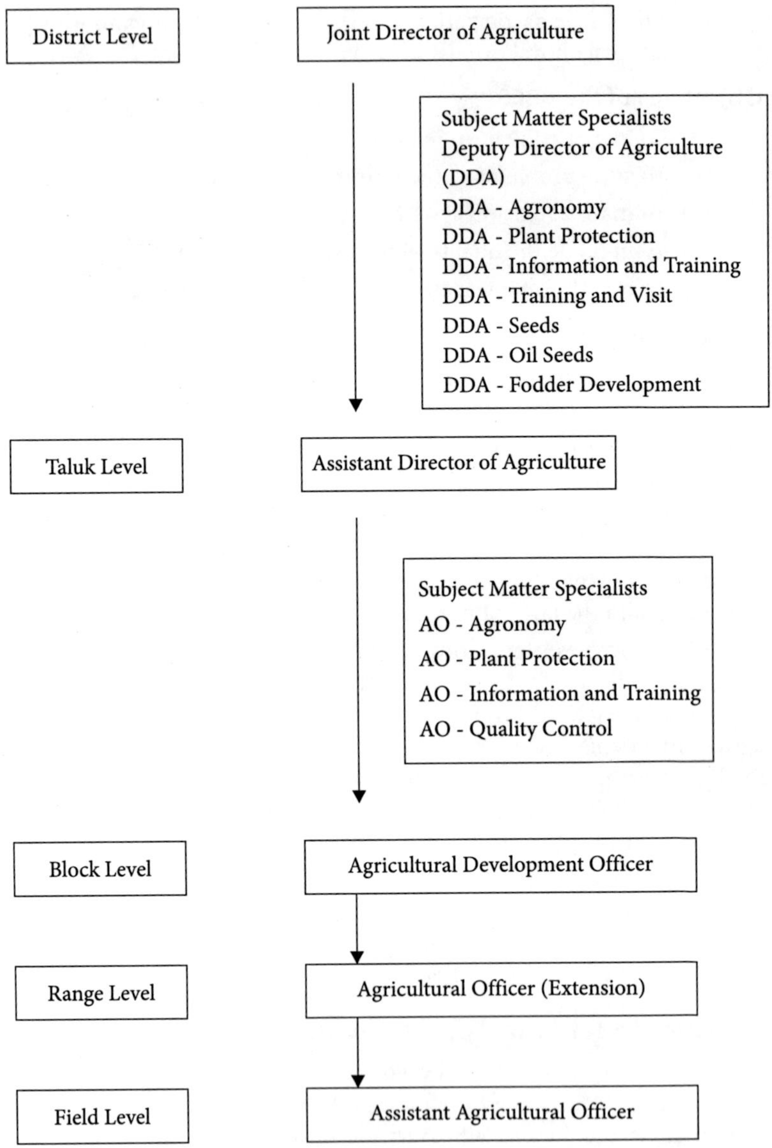

Organizational Pattern of BBES

(1990-92) in Pollachi division of Coimbatore district, Tamil Nadu in close collaboration with the extension functionaries of the Departments of Agriculture, Animal Husbandry, Forestry and Sericulture and scientists of TNAU.

Definition

Satellite Model Farm may be of any size, diversified over a period of time with a combination of compatible, feasible, profitable and eco-friendly agriculture related enterprises by the farmers blending their experience and wisdom with the technologies developed by the research system and received from Government and non-Government development organizations to serve as a learning and training ground for farmers, extension personnel as well as scientists for promoting the diffusion of integrated farming system technologies to client system.

Objectives of Satellite Model Farm Approach/Concept

(i) To ensure Man-Land-Crop-Animal Ecosystem relationship for sustainable Agriculture.

(ii) To educate and motivate farmers for farm diversification by resorting to compatible, profitable, feasible and eco-friendly combination of agriculture and allied enterprises.

(iii) To enhance maximum utilization of resources available in the farm, home and environment.

(iv) To increase the competency of extension personnel to perform the whole-role of transferring crop based as well as allied enterprises technology.

(v) To strengthen the linkages and coordination within and among the clients, extension and research systems.

(vi) To promote planning from below and Participatory Technology Development (PTD).

(vii) To identify Model Satellite Farms for providing experiential learning and interaction among farmers, extension workers and scientists.

(viii) To render cost effective quality extension work to the client system.

(ix) To give opportunity for the scientists to better understand the appropriateness and the level of performance of the recommended technologies under a given farming situation.

(x) To increase employment and income generating activities within the farm/village.

(xi) To create scope for the establishment of viable agrobased industries at block/village level itself in the long run.

(xii) To improve the overall standard of living of the rural folk.

Satellite Model Farm: An Overview

As per the stipulated criteria, one farm with a particular combination of enterprises already existing is selected in a segment of each block. A team of extension workers drawn from agriculture and other line departments along with a group of neighbouring farmers irrespective of their farm size and farm diversification, study the existing combination, make recommendations for improving the productivity of each enterprise, analyze the existing resources and suggest suitable and feasible additional enterprises. The satellite farmer can also be encouraged to interact with the visiting neighbouring farmers. The selected farmer is to be regularly contacted by the team of extension workers to render technical assistance in a holistic manner rather than each extension worker of a particular department meeting the farmer separately and giving recommendations in a piece meal manner. Consequently, the selected farm becomes a model satellite farm from where the concept of proven diversification of farming radiates to the neighbouring farms through the target group discussions conducted in the satellite model farm for neighbouring farmers. Motivated by the possibilities of diversification of farming through personal experience and interaction with satellite farmer, fellow farmers, extension workers and scientists, the neighbouring farmers come forward for diversification. Subsequently, the teams of extension workers make follow up visits and render all possible guidance to develop the farms of these neighbouring farmers also to serve as satellite model farms.

Advantages of SMFA

(i) An eye-opener for promoting the integrated land use at farm level.

(ii) Facilitates desirable farmer-farmer-extension worker-scientist interaction.

(iii) Provides greater scope to extension workers and farmers for experiential learning.

(iv) Creates congenial atmosphere for better coordination among the line departments at the farm level.

(v) Serves as a model farm not only to the farmers and extension workers but also to the scientists.

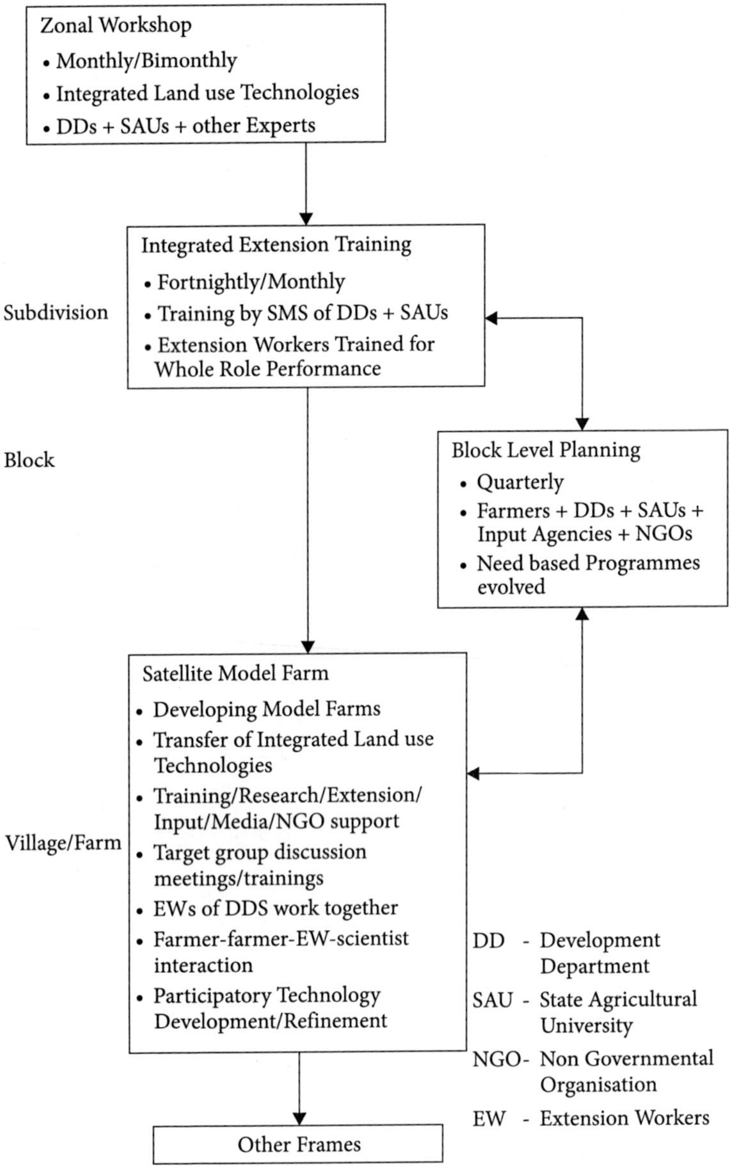

Satellite Model Farm Approach : A Schematic Framework

(vi) Gives opportunities to study and understand interdisciplinary and inter enterprises technology behaviour.

(vii) Enables to identify and understand the use of Indigenous Technical Knowledge (ITK).

(viii) Helps the extension workers and scientists to get first hand knowledge about the problems faced by the farmers.

(ix) Provides opportunities for the exchange of experiences of farmers about the profitable combination of enterprises.

(x) Helps the farmers to develop their own skill in choosing the appropriate combination of enterprises.

(xi) Creates a cooperative attitude among the farmers for better production and marketing of various agricultural produces.

(xii) Minimizes the risk in adopting a single enterprise.

(xiii) Provides ample opportunities for the involvement of NGOs and other supporting agencies.

(xiv) Helps extension workers to render farm based, need based and eco-friendly recommendations to the farmers.

(xv) It ensures cost effective quality extension work.

FOR DISCUSSION

1. What is ASA? Elaborate the elements of ASA with examples.
2. Write down the advantages of ASA in management.
3. Define BBES. Discuss how does it differ from T&V system?
4. Explain the principles, scope and advantages of BBES.
5. What is Satellite Model Farm Approach?
6. What is the important significance of SMFA?
7. Discuss SMFA with suitable examples.

16

Management of Training and Development

Managing Technology, Media and Audience

Technology means application of science to the practical aims of human life.

Appropriate technology means a low cost technology using mainly local/easily available materials and skills to meet a recognized need.

For managing media the following points need to be considered:

Real time requirement (how timely the information should be).

Frequency requirement (how often the information must be available or furnished).

Accuracy requirement (how detailed or correct the information must be).

Data reduction requirement (where the information must be supplied).

Storage requirement (where the information must be stored).

With respect to agriculture, the audience is farmers. The management principles can be used for managing the audience. Adoption of technology by the farmer is not an end in itself. Return from the farm which may be in the form of produce or money is crucial for the farmer, as it depends to the extent to which the farmer could meet the goals of the family.

Management of Transfer of Technology (ToT)

ToT refers to the entire process of technology development, processing, dissemination and integration through research, extension and farming systems keeping in view the resources, organizational limitations and capabilities to solve the problems of the society.

Technologies must be developed keeping in view farmers existing practices, resources, environment and preferences. Technologies must provide solutions to farmers' problems.

Communication of technologies alone is not enough. The other aspects, infrastructure, support services policy, marketing, input training, etc. must be assured for effective utilization.

Creation of awareness and equip both farmers and scientists to work together to generate technologies appropriate to the local situation.

Management Training and Development Techniques

Training is concerned with imparting with specific skills for particular purposes. It is a process of educating a person so as to make him fit, qualified and proficient in doing some job.

The term development refets broadly to the nature and direction of change induced among employees through the process of training and education.

Training for Lower Level Management

The method to be used in a particular case depends on the number of trainees, nature of work and facilities available for training.

(i) ***On the Job Training:*** The worker is trained by his immediate supervisor or by an experienced employee in real work situation. The trainee is explained the method of handling tools, operating the machines, etc.

(ii) ***Vestibule Training:*** Employees are trained in a special training center within the plant. An attempt is made to duplicate as nearly as possible the actual conditions of the work place. Qualified instructors under carefully planned and controlled learning conditions provide the training.

(iii) ***Apprenticeship Training:*** Usually combine on the job training and classroom instruction in particular subjects. The trainees serve as apprentices under the direct supervision of experts for a long period and some stipend is paid to them during the training period.

(iv) ***Classroom Training:*** Theoretical instructions are provided to the trainees through the joint efforts of employers and educational institutions. Employers send their employees for training to the technical or vocational training institutes. Special courses are designed to fill the needs of the organization and lecture method is used for instruction.

Training and Development Techniques

(i) ***Lecture:*** It consists of oral presentation of information along with the help of teaching aids so as to help the listeners to understand the concept, principle and method being presented.

(ii) ***Demonstration:*** It is a presentation, which illustrates a task, a procedure or the use of equipment in a step-by-step fashion so that trainees can observe and understand the principle, procedure in an interesting and convincing way.

(iii) ***Brain Storming:*** It is a group based creativity technique designed to encourage lateral thinking around a stated question or problem. It will result in generation of a large number of ideas to solve a problem.

(iv) ***Group Discussion:*** Refers to exchange of ideas and thoughts by two or more people on a selected topic. It may be related to clarification of ideas or help in understanding and application of ideas to practical situation:

- **(a)** ***Seminar:*** Different aspects of a particular subjects are discussed in a logical sequence under the guidance of experts and experienced professionals. Its purpose is to pool thes expertise of different professionals and come out with conclusions.
- **(b)** ***Workshop:*** Refers to assembly of interested and selected group of people to learn and practise specific skills under experienced professional guidance. A mix of theory and practical is provided.
- **(c)** ***Symposium:*** It is a gathering of experts who present their findings or ideas on a specific sub-topic related to a major subject. The output may result in the publication of edited papers presented by the experts.
- **(d)** ***Syndicate:*** Group of people (8-10) assigned with a task of investigating a particular problem and to find out the solution. A chairperson and a secretary coordinate it.
- **(e)** ***Panel discussion:*** Discussion of any particular topic by a panel of 3- 5 experts representing different areas of the same subject.

(v) ***Simulation Methods:*** It consists of simulating real life experiences.

- **(a)** ***Role-play:*** Technique where one or group of trainees enacts a real life situation which helps the participants to experience the true feelings of that situation. The actors of a play are expected to behave as if it were a real life situation.
- **(b)** ***In basket exercises:*** They are the simulation that create a complex work organization, rotate participant through key roles in it and have them deal with specific simulation of a kind they encounter in real life.

(c) ***Game:*** It is a structured activity in which two or more participants compete within constraints of rule to achieve an objective.

(vi) ***Case Study:*** Consists of materials related to an event or problem. Since most of the case studies are related to real life situation, an analysis of case studies will help in acquiring development of analytical skills. The trainees are presented with cases either through written materials or video and are requested to analyze different situations and make their own decisions.

(vii) ***Open Learning:*** There is a greater amount of freedom in choice of topics and duration of study. It offers opportunities to study from workplace or home. Training and evaluation is learner centred and aim at imparting practical skills and knowledge to them.

(a) Audio cassette
(b) Video
(c) Interactive video
(d) Computer-based training
(e) CD-ROM
(f) Internet

Advantages of Training and Development

(i) Check wastage of resources both materials and non-materials.
(ii) Increase efficiency, productivity and create better standards.
(iii) Enhance confidence, ability and morale of the trainees and trainers.
(iv) Improve motivation of the participants and help them to become creative.
(v) Bring behavioural changes in terms of attitude, knowledge and skill.

FOR DICSUSSION

1. Define training.
2. Discuss the methods of managing technology, media and audience.
3. Explain the different methods of training.
4. Discuss the role of information technology in training.
5. What are the advantages of training and development?

17

Management Tools

Management tools are very useful in organization for achieving the organizational objectives as per the plans. The following are the some of the tools which are extensively used in organization.

1. SWOT Analysis

SWOT analysis is an extremely useful tool for understanding and decision making for all sorts of situations in business and organizations. SWOT is an acronym for Strengths, Weaknesses, Opportunities and Threats. These four attributes are also called SWOT parameters.

Strengths

It is the basic asset of the organization that would provide competitive advantage for its growth and development, *e.g.* patents, strong brand names, good reputation among customers, cost advantages from proprietary know-how, exclusive access to high natural resources, favourable access to distribution networks.

What advantages do you have?

What do you do well?

What relevant resources do you have access to?

What do other people see as your strengths?

Consider this from your own point of view and from the point of view of the people you deal with. Don't be modest. Be realistic. If you are having any difficulty with this, try writing down a list of your characteristics. Some of these will hopefully be strengths.

In looking at your strengths, think about them in relation to your competitors—for example, if all your competitors provide high quality products, then a high quality production process is not a strength in the market, it is a necessity.

Weaknesses

Absence of certain strengths may be viewed as a weakness. It is the liability of an organization that can create a state of time and situation specific disadvantage for its growth and development, e.g. lack of patent protection, a weak brand name, poor reputation among customers, high cost structure, lack of access to the best natural resources, lack of access to key distribution channels.

What could you improve?

What do you do badly?

What should you avoid?

Again, consider this from an internal and external basis: do other people seem to perceive weaknesses that you do not see? Are your competitors doing any better than you? It is best to be realistic now, and face any unpleasant truths as soon as possible.

Opportunities

It is the ability of the organization to grow and achieve its specific objectives in a given situation, *e.g.* an unfulfilled customer needs arrival of new technologies, loosening of regulations and removal of international trade barriers.

Where are the good opportunities facing you?

What are the interesting trends you are aware of?

Useful opportunities can come from such things as:

Changes in technology and markets on both, a broad and a narrow scale.

Changes in Government policy related to your field.

Changes in social patterns, population profiles, lifestyle changes, etc.

Local events.

A useful application to looking to opportunities is to look at your strengths and ask yourself whether these open up any opportunities. Alternatively, look at your weaknesses and ask yourself whether you could open up opportunities by eliminating them.

Threats

It is a situation that blocks the abilities of the organization to grow and develop for meeting its ultimate goal, e.g. shifts in consumer tastes away from the firm's products, emergence of substitute products, new regulations, increased trade barriers. What obstacles do you face?

What is your competitor doing?

Are the required specifications for your job, products or services changing?

Is changing technology threatening your position?

Do you have bad debt or cash-flow problems?

Could any of your weaknesses seriously threaten your business?

Carrying out this analysis will often be illumination—both in terms of pointing out what needs to be done, and in putting problems into perspective. Strength and weaknesses are the corporate, organizational characteristics in nature which are internal. Opportunity and threat are external in nature.

Internal	External
Share holders	Government,
Employees	Customers
Product qualities	Economics/political situation
Price of the product	Pricing policy of the government

Example of SWOT

A start-up small consultancy business might carry out the following SWOT analysis:

Strengths

We are above to respond very quickly as we have no red tape, no need for higher management approval, etc.

We are able to give really good customer care, as the current small amount of work means we have plenty of time to devote to customers.

Our lead consultant has strong reputation within the market.

We can change direction quickly if we find that our marketing is not working.

We have little overhead charges so we can offer good value to customers.

Weaknesses

Our company has to market prestige or reputation.

We have a small staff with shallow skills base in many areas.

We are vulnerable to vital staff being sick, leaving, etc.

Our cash flow will be unreliable in the early stages.

Opportunities

Our business sector is expanding with many future opportunities for success.

Our local council wants to encourage local businesses with work where possible.

Our competitors may be slow to adopt new technologies.

Threats

Will developments in technology change this market beyond our ability to adapt?

A small change in focus of a large competitor might wipe out any market position we achieve.

The consultancy might therefore decide to specialize in rapid response, good value services to local businesses. Marketing would be in selected local publications, to get the greatest possible market presence for a set advertising budget. The consultancy should keep up-to-date with changes in technology where possible.

Uses of SWOT analysis

(i) It plays an important role in understanding the management problems at all stages irrespective of the type of organization.

(ii) It helps in taking appropriate decisions for the development of an organization in a particular operational environment.

(iii) It is useful for increasing competitive abilities of scientists and organizations.

(iv) It helps to bring out the relevant changes in projects and organizations.

(v) It gives the scope for safety and security to every organization without facing hurdles in running the organization profitably.

(vi) SWOT analysis is a framework for analyzing your strengths and weaknesses and the opportunities and threats you face.

(vii) It helps to focus on your strengths, minimize weaknesses and take the greatest possible advantage of opportunities available.

Applications of SWOT

Here are some examples of what a SWOT analysis can be used to assess:

(i) *Industry:* Many industrial scientists, managers and technical personnel applied the SWOT analysis frequently on systems and organizations for taking appropriate decisions for their smooth running. SWOT application was first used in 1910 in European and other developed countries.

(ii) *Strategic Management/Planning:* It is a continuous process of effectively relating the organizations objectives and resources to the opportunities in the environment. SWOT analysis helps policy makers and managers in shaping the strategic directions of a specific agency operating within a given situation/context.

Besides industry, the SWOT analysis in general is applicable in many walks of life:

- Individual
- Household/families
- Private organizations
- Government organizations
- Politics
- A company (its position in the market, commercial viability, etc.)
- A method of sales distribution
- A product or brand
- A business idea
- A strategic option, such as entering a new market or launching a new product
- An opportunity to make an acquisition
- A potential partnership
- Changing a supplier
- Outsourcing a service, activity or resource
- An investment opportunity

SWOT Analysis Example I

Strengths

- Advantages of proposition
- Capabilities
- Competitive advantages
- USP's (unique selling points)
- Resources, assets, people
- Experience, knowledge, data

Financial reserves, likely returns
Marketing—reach, distribution, awareness
Innovative aspects
Location and geographical
Price, value, quality
Accreditations, qualifications, certification
Processes, systems, IT, communications
Cultural, attitudinal, behavioural
Management cover, succession

Weaknesses

Disadvantages of proposition
Gaps in capabilities
Lack of competitive strength
Reputation, presence and reach
Financials
Own known vulnerabilities
Timescales, deadlines and pressures
Cash flow, start-up cash-drain
Continuity, supply chain robustness
Effects on core activities distraction
Reliability of data, plan predictability
Morale, commitment, leadership
Accreditations, etc.
Processes and systems, etc.
Management cover, succession

Opportunities

Market developments
Competitors' vulnerabilities
Industry or lifestyle trends
Technology development and innovation
Global influences
New markets, vertical, horizontal
Niche target markets
Geographical, export, import

New USP's
Tactics—surprise, major contracts, etc.
Business and product development
Information and research
Partnerships, agencies, distribution
Volumes, production, economies
Seasonal, weather, fashion influences

Threats

Political effects
Legislative effects
Environmental effects
IT developments
Competitor intentions—various
Market demand
New technologies, services, ideas
Vital contracts and partners
Sustaining internal capabilities
Obstacles faced
Insurmountable weaknesses
Loss of key staff
Sustainable financial backing
Economy—home, abroad
Seasonality, weather effects

SWOT Analysis Example II

The SWOT analysis example is based on an imaginary situation. The scenario is based on a business-to-business manufacturing company, who historically rely on distributors to take their products to the end user market. The opportunity, and therefore the subject for the SWOT analysis, is for the manufacturer to create a new company of its own to distribute its products direct to certain end-user sectors, which are not being covered or developed by its normal distributors.

Subject

The creation of own distributor company to access new end-user sectors not currently being developed.

Strengths

End-use sales control and direction.

Right products, quality and reliability.

Superior product performance vs competitors.

Better product life and durability.

Spare manufacturing capacity.

Some staff have experience of end-user sector.

Have customer lists.

Direct delivery capability.

Product innovations ongoing.

Can serve from existing sites.

Products have required accreditations.

Processes and IT should cope.

Management is committed and confident.

Weakness

Customer lists not tested.

Some gaps in range for certain sectors.

We would be a small player.

No direct marketing experience.

We cannot supply end-users abroad.

Need more sales people.

Limited budget.

No pilot or trial done yet.

Don't have a detailed plan yet.

Delivery-staff need training.

Customer service staff need training.

Processes and systems, etc.

Management cover insufficient.

Opportunities

Could develop new products.

Local competitors have poor products.

Profit margins will be good.

End-users respond to new ideas.

Could extend to overseas.

New specialist applications.

Can surprise competitors.

Support core business economies.

Could seek better supplier deals.

Threats

Legislation could impact.

Environmental effects would favour larger competitors.

Existing core business distribution risk.

Market demand very seasonal.

Retention of key staff critical.

Could distract from core business.

Possible negative publicity.

Vulnerable to reactive attack by major competitors.

2. Personal Effectiveness: Johari Window

In an organization the manager has to deal with human beings for obtaining the objectives so the personal effectiveness is very useful for the success of management. Although one precondition for personal effectiveness is better self-awareness, understanding one does not alone make a person effective.

The Johari Window

One simple model for self-awareness that is widely used is the Johari Window, developed by Joseph Luft and Harry Ingham (Luft, 1973). In this model, there are two main dimensions for understanding the self : those aspects of a person's behaviour and style that are known to him (self) and those aspects of his behaviour known to those with whom he interacts (others). A combination of these two dimensions reveals four areas of knowledge about the self.

Johari Window

	Known to self	Not known to self
Known to others	Arena	Blind
Not known to others	Closed	Dark

The upper left-hand square is the arena of the public self-that part of an individual's behaviour known both to the person and to others with whom he interacts. The arena includes information such as name, age, physical appearance and familial or organization affiliation.

The blind area contains those aspects of the person's behaviour and style that others know but that the person himself does not. A person may have mannerisms of which he is not aware that are perceived by others as funny, annoying, or pleasing. For example, an individual might be surprised to hear that his method of asking questions annoys others because it is interpreted as cross-examination rather than curiosity or a request for information.

The closed area involves that which is known to the person but not revealed to others; things in this area are secret. For example, a subordinate may be annoyed if his supervisor does not ask him to sit down during a meeting, but he will remain standing without letting the supervisor know that he is annoyed. The supervisor may think that the subordinate does not mind standing and accept his behaviour as apart of their hierarchical relationship. Most of the people have many such feelings in their closed areas that they are unwilling to reveal to the persons concerned.

The fourth area is the dark area, inaccessible both to the person and to others. Some psychologists believe that this is a very large area indeed and those certain circumstances (for example, an accident), particular life stage, or special techniques such as psychoanalysis or psychodynamics may suddenly make a person realize some hidden aspects of himself. Because the dark area cannot be consciously controlled or changed and therefore cannot be considered in a discussion of personal effectiveness, this discussion will be limited to the arena, blind and closed areas.

Personal-Effectiveness

Although it might be assumed that a large arena and small blind and closed areas would be desirable and would contribute to personal effectiveness, this is not necessarily so, a person with a large arena may still be ineffective because a large arena is not the only factor in effectiveness.

Possible Effectiveness Combinations

By combining high or low effectiveness with large or small area in the arena and the blind and closed areas gives twelve possible personality combinations as shown below:

Arena	Blind Area	Closed Area	Effectiveness	Type of Person
	Large		High	Self-Confident
	Large		Low	Unperceptive
	Small		High	Perceptive
	Small		Low	Overly Cautions
		Large	High	Good Listener
		Large	Low	Secretive
		Small	High	Frank
		Small	Low	Egocentric
Small			High	Task-Oriented
Small			Low	Closed
Large			Low	Superficial
Large			High	Open

Self-Confident

A person with a large blind area and high effectiveness is likely to be self-confident. He may not be aware of his limitations, but he may also not be aware of some of his strengths. However, he is likely to rely on his strengths and be blind to his weaknesses. Although his effectiveness may see him through situations, it will certainly be limited because of his lack of awareness of some of his limitations and strengths.

Unperceptive

A person with a large blind area and low effectiveness is unperceptive to the non-verbal cues that people may send about his behaviour. For example, a professor who cannot see that the whole class is drowsy from a dull lecture may continue to bore the class. Unperceptive people find it difficult to understand subtle sarcasm, subdued communication of resentment and negative feelings, and body language.

Perceptive

A person with a small blind area and with high effectiveness is quite perceptive of verbal and non-verbal cues. This perceptiveness helps him to pick up such cues quickly and use them to change his strategy of interaction and hence his effectiveness. A perceptive supervisor who sees that a subordinate is pre-occupied with some problem asks the subordinate about what is bothering him before pursuing task-related topics. This is likely to help the subordinate become more open and relate to the supervisor more effectively.

Overly Cautions

A person with a smaller blind area knows more about his strengths and his limitations. However, if such a person has low effectiveness he is more likely to be overly concerned with his weaknesses than he is to concentrate on his strengths. An over cautious person finds it difficult to take the initiative and to risk because his limitations loom large to him and may immobilize him. Just having a smaller blind area does not necessarily make a person effective.

Good Listener

A person with a large closed area and with high effectiveness is likely to be a good listener. Instead of giving his own opinions, he listens to the opinions of others and makes decisions based on his own judgment. He may not share his own point of view, even if his views are not close to the views of others.

Secretive

A person with a large closed area and with low effectiveness is likely to be secretive. Other people may wonder what criteria he uses to judge them or what he expects from them. They are also not likely to know how he feels, as he will not share his feelings with others.

Frank

A person with a small closed area and with high effectiveness is likely to be quite outspoken and frank. He gives feedback and expresses his opinion and points of view without any inhibition. He shares his personal feelings, experiences, joys and sorrows as well.

Egocentric

A person with a small closed area but with low effectiveness may tend to talk excessively about himself, his achievements, his talents, his experiences, and even his personal life. He is so egocentric that he is not likely to pay attention to others and their needs.

Task-oriented

A person with a small arena can be quite effective in a limited way. One model for an effective administrator is a person with a small arena and a high task orientation. Such a person does not relate to others on a personal or social level. He is mainly concerned with task performance and may restrict his communication and interaction with others only to the tasks involved.

Closed

A person with a small arena and low effectiveness is usually closed, neither sharing his impressions nor listening to others and using the feedback he receives. Such a person will be quite ineffective.

Superficial

A person with a large arena but with low effectiveness does not use his openness to good effect with others. He may interact with others, offer his opinions, and listen to others, but these acts are usually of a superficial nature. He does not exercise his judgments about when to open and what to look for in the feedback he receives from others.

Open

A person with a large arena (the open self) and high effectiveness is open. His opinions are given freely and are well understood, he feels free to communicate his impressions, and he gives feedback to others with sensitivity that they appreciate. Similarly, he is eager to receive feedback from others: he solicits it and then critically examines and uses it to good effect.

Developing Personal Effectiveness

Personal effectiveness must be viewed across three dimensions: openness, perceptiveness and communication, all significant dimensions in interpersonal relationships. By becoming more open, a person reduces his closed area; the blind area is reduced by increasing perceptiveness: and communication can be improved in various ways. These three dimensions, however, do not function in isolation: each interacts with the others. In order to increase effectiveness, it is necessary to work on a combination of all three.

Openness: It is the extent to which one shares ideas, feelings, experiences, impressions, perceptions and various other personal data with others. It is an important quality and contributes a great deal to a person's effectiveness.

Perceptiveness: The ability to pick up verbal and non-verbal cues from others indicates perceptiveness. This should be combined with other two dimensions. It can be increased by checking with others about their reactions to what has been said. If a person does not do this he may become overly concerned about the cues he receives.

Communication: It is an important dimension to increase the personal effectiveness and it should be combined with the other two for higher effectiveness.

3. Participatory Rural Appraisal (PRA)

PRA came about as a research approach by late 1980s. The term PRA was first used in 1988. It is a continuation of Rapid Rural Appraisal (RRA). Mr. Robert Chamber is considered as the pioneer in evolving PRA approaches. Before the advent of these approaches questionnaires and survey methods were followed for analyzing rural situation, which were costly and time consuming.

It is a methodology for interacting with villagers, understanding them and learning from them. The process of involving local people in the analysis and interpretation of a rural situation. PRA is a means of collecting different kinds of data, identifying and mobilizing intended group and evoking their participation and also opening ways in which intended groups can participate in decision making, project design, implementation and monitoring.

Definition

It is a semistrucutred way of learning relatively quickly and in a multidisciplinary team from local people about the key problems and opportunities of an area and of deciding on an agreed set of possibilities for alleviating the problems and or mapping good use of the opportunities.

It is a method of involving the rural people in all the stages of programme planning starting from the analysis of the situation to the final evaluation of the programme to which the programme is meant. This method is highly suitable to the villages which are having less than 1000 farm families.

Aim

Participatory Rural Appraisal aims at enabling the rural people in analyzing their past, examining their present and envisaging their future by assessing their socio-economic and geographic situation, identifying their problems, exploring their locally available resources, hammering out feasible solutions and formulating action plans realisable during a certain time span (Narayanaswamy and Boraian, 1993).

Principles of PRA

(i) Participation

(ii) Triangulation.

(iii) Approximation.

(iv) On the spot analysis.

(v) Respecting of views of others.
(vi) Listen more, speak less.
(vii) Embracing errors.
(viii) Diagnosis and solutions.
(ix) Building rapport with the people.
(x) Openness.
(xi) Cost effective approach.
(xii) Accepting creativity of others.

Scope of PRA

(i) To assess local condition and social relationship.
(ii) To assess natural resources inventory.
(iii) To identify problems.
(iv) To identify priority of needs and programmes.
(v) To appraise of emergency.
(vi) To gather data for decision making.
(vii) To appraise project feasibility.
(viii) To assess project impact.
(ix) To generate new project proposal.
(x) To formulate and test hypothesis.
(xi) To prepare farm plan.
(xii) To validate/cross check existing information.
(xiii) To find the utility and changes overtime.
(xiv) To quantify the data.

Steps to Conduct PRA

(i) Introduce purpose
(ii) Explain the method
(iii) Observe the farmers and how they participate
(iv) Use check list
(v) Critically follow discussions
(vi) Distinguish facts, opinions and rumours
(vii) Conclude the session
(viii) Discuss and analyze with officials

PRA Tools and Techniques

PRA techniques are both an analysis tool for decision making as well as a capacity building tool for community resource use and management for improved livelihood.

The purpose is to provide the community with understanding of their natural resources, their constraints, problems and opportunities.

PRA-Tools and Techniques	
1. Transect and Walk	17. Farming Household Map
2. Social Map	18. Technology Assessment Index
3. Resource Map	19. Sustainability Analysis Index
4. Agro-ecology Map	20. Flow Diagram
5. Technology Map	21. Venn Diagramming
6. Mobility Map	22. Socio Economic and Gender Analysis (SEAGA)
7. Time Line	23. Need Assessment
8. Time Trend	24. Consequence Analysis
9. Seasonal Calendar	25. Daily Routine and Activity Diagram
10. Impact Diagram	26. SWOT Analysis
11. Wealth Ranking	27. Problem Identification, Problem Tree and Action Plan
12. ITK Map	28. Bio-Resource Flow Model
13. Livelihood Analysis	29. Flowcharts
14. Matrix Scoring	30. Socio-gram
15. Climatic Diagram	31. Demographic Profile
16. Professional Ranking	

Steps to Organize PRA

(i) Any special appointments required.
(ii) Selection of specific sites.
(iii) Good preparation of questionnaires.
(iv) Careful approach of informants.
(v) Keep materials available.

Social and Communication Skills of PRA

(i) Explain the purpose of your visit.
(ii) Be related.
(iii) Insist on informality.

(iv) Listen carefully.

(v) Probe a topic.

(vi) Encourage everybody to take part in the exercise and discussion and to share knowledge.

(vii) Show respect.

(viii) Pay attention to reactions of other people present.

Advantages of PRA

(i) Helps to develop capabilities of groups of people for critical analysis and assessment of their rural situation.

(ii) Better planning and village profiling.

(iii) Quick identification of problems.

(iv) Quick rapport building with villagers.

(v) Ensure more involvement and participation of the villagers in programme development.

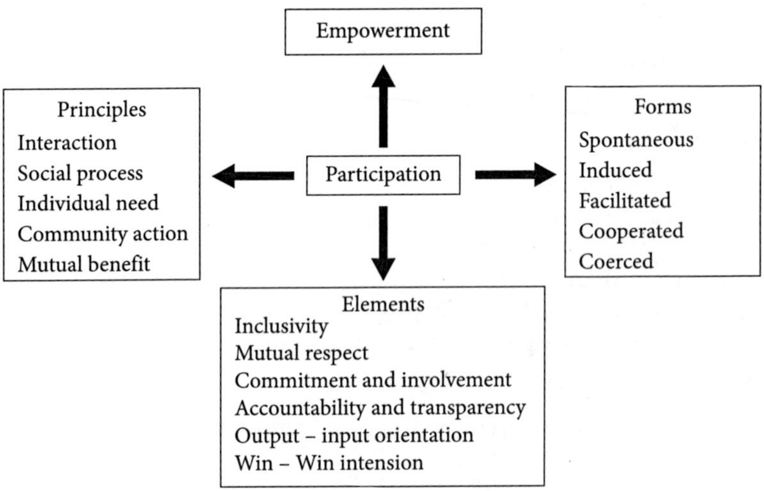

Concept of Participation

(vi) Local resources are used in the techniques.

(vii) Make bureaucracy sensitive to the needs of the people.

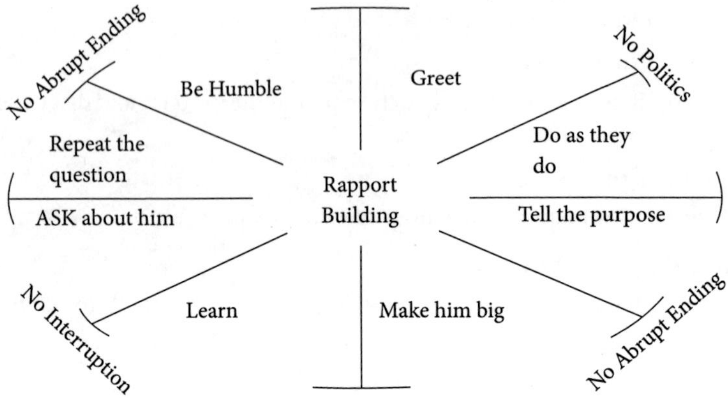

Practical utility of PRA

(i) As a participatory alternative in development and research.
(ii) As a set of principles.
(iii) As a set of data gathering and awareness raising tool.
(iv) As a method of participatory project management.
(v) As a tool for addressing specific issues.
(vi) As a work in progress.

Agro Eco-System Analysis (AESA)

Agro Eco-System Analysis is comprehensive analysis of the land, its biophysical and ecological productivity, feasibility, sustainability with due attention for socio-economic feasibility, acceptability and the impact it generates. AESA is a process to learn how to observe the crop, analyze the field situation and to make proper decisions for crop management involving a multidisciplinary approach.

Objectives of AESA

(i) Analysis of agro eco-system using multidisciplinary and systems approach
(ii) Developing suitable indicators for monitoring and evaluation
(iii) Developing a sustainable decision support system for efficient crises management in agro ecosystem.

Transactional Analysis

Transactional Analysis (or TA as it is often called) is a model of people and relationships that was developed during the 1960s by Dr. Eric Berne. It is based on two notions:

First that we have three parts or 'ego-states' to our 'personality. The other assumption is that these converse with one another in 'transactions' (hence the name).

TA is a way of looking at what goes on between people and inside people. It can explain human situations in a way that gives insight into what is happening in a current interaction.

Transactional analysis has an optimistic view of human nature that believes that people can change despite life's events and that it is never too late to change one's life. All decisions that are made in life can be redecided (Gladding, 1996).

TA is widely used in

Management,

Education,

Politics,

Religion,

Training,

Counselling,

Psychotherapy, and

Psychiatry.

Transactional analysis uses seven methods to analyze and predict behavior

1. **Structural analysis** looks at what is happening within the individual (Study of ego states).
2. **Transactional analysis** looks at what is happening between two or more people (Interaction between people).
3. **Life positions**—self-confidence and confidence in others.
4. **Strokes**—Recognition of another's presence.
5. **Stamps**—The study of collection of feelings.
6. **Time structuring**—Ways of spending time.
7. **Script analysis** looks at the life plan the individual has chosen to follow (Study of life plan).

1. Structural Analysis

1. Structural Analysis describes each person in terms of three ego states: Parent, Adult, and Child
2. Parent ego state gives advice, discipline, protects, nurtures, keeps tradition as and makes rules about how life should be.

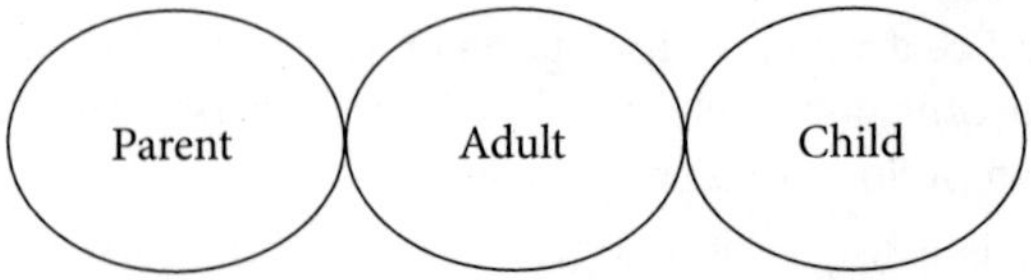

3. Adult ego state contains the objective, thinking, rational and logical ability to deal with reality
4. Child ego state is the source of childlike behaviors and feelings

Ego states

While all the people are structurally alike, in that all have a PAC (Parent, Adult and Child), they differ in content differences and functional differences. Differing people will be dominated by one ego state or the other. A normal person will have a proper balance between the ego states and will possess flexibility to move from one to another depending on the situation. Ideally PAC are separate but in many people P or C tend to contaminate A. This results in persons having prejudices and delusions.

2. Analysing Transactions

Transaction is a unit of social interaction which consists of a stimulus by one person and a response by another. The purpose of analyzing transactions is to identify which part of a person— P or A or C is originating each stimulus and response. Transactions may be verbal or non verbal. They can also be classified as complimentary, crossed and ulterior transactions. Complementary or open or parallel transactions are those in which stimulus and response on P-A-C diagram made parallel lines. E.g.

Teacher: "You should have done your home work". Student: "I am sorry. I will do tomorrow"	Illustrated in figure

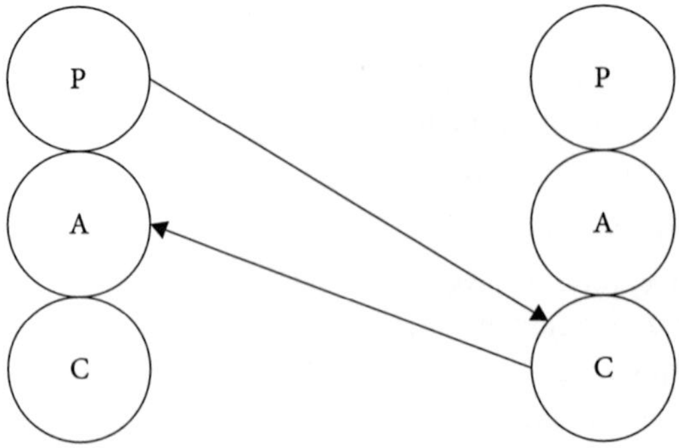

3. Life Positions

Another TA concept is that people have chosen basic attitudes towards themselves and others, either positive or negative, or to put it more colloquially: Each person's perception is that either I'm OK or Not-OK, and You are either OK or Not-OK. Here 'I am Ok-You are OK' is the ideal, healthy and constructive position in which people feel good about themselves and others. This position is reached as a result of conscious decision of the individual.

4. Strokes

A STROKE is a single unit of recognition between two people. Strokes can be verbal or non-verbal, positive or negative, and of varying degrees of intensity. It is an act of other's presence. They serve as a unit of motivation. A pleasant smile to a colleague or statement like 'I like you'

Berne observed that people need strokes, the units of interpersonal recognition, to survive and thrive. Understanding how people give and receive positive and negative strokes and changing unhealthy patterns of stroking are powerful aspects of work in transactional analysis.

5. Stamps

At the end of a transaction, the feelings get collected which are referred to 'stamps' in T.A. terminology. When sufficient number of stamps are collected they are usually encashed for a 'prize'. There are two types of stamps. They are Gold stamps and Grey stamps. Former are collection of good and positive feelings while latter consist of bad and negative feelings. Every one collects grey stamps at one time or other. It is paramount of importance to learn how to give up grey stamps and collect gold stamps. A person with healthy personality will also give gold stamps to others and also refrain from giving hurts, insults etc. which results in grey stamps in others.

6. Time structuring

Strokes are essential for all of us. One can get the desired strokes by structuring one's time properly.

Berne identifies six classifications for the short-term structuring of time:

Withdrawal: This is the case at one extreme. People do not communicate, individuals remain wrapped in their own thoughts. This might be the case on the bus, on in a doctor's waiting room.

Rituals: Fixed and socially approved ways of behaving towards other people. E.g.

'Morning,' how are you?'—'All right thanks. How are you?' and so on.

Activities: These are normally goal directed behaviour like work, hobbies etc. The transactions are determined by the material being dealt with—concrete, wood, mathematical problems etc.—and are typically Adult-to-Adult.

Pastimes: These transactions are generally very formulaic, like rituals, but less stylized and predictable. They're the kind of thing we might come across at a party or similar social event.

Games: Recurring transactions with concealed motivation progressing to predictable outcome. People play games to get strokes, to strengthen one's life positions.

Intimacy: Honest, open, loving and trusting relationship.

7. Life Script

Eric Berne proposed that dysfunctional behavior is the result of self-limiting decisions made in childhood in the interest of survival.

Such decisions culminate in what Berne called the "life script," the pre-conscious life plan that governs the way life is lived out. Changing the life script is the aim of transactional analysis psychotherapy. For change to occur, one must be aware of oneself and then choose more successful pathways.

Reference

1. Berne, E., 1964, Games people play. The Psychology of Human Relations, Grower Press, New York.
2. Mitchell, T.R., 1978, People in organization understanding their behaviour, McGraw Hill Book Company, New York.
3. Singh, Nirmal, 2000, Principles of management, Theory, practices and techniques. Deep and Deep Publications, New Delhi-27.

FOR DISCUSSION

1. What do you mean by SWOT and how does it use for management?
2. Write down your strength, weakness, opportunity and threat and discuss for your improvement.
3. What is Johari Window? Discuss the four dimensions of Johari Window.
4. What are all the points to be considered for increasing the personal effectiveness?
5. Discuss PRA and its Aim, Scope and Advantages of PRA.
6. Discuss the principles and steps involved in conducting PRA.
7. Discuss the tools used for conducting PRA.
8. What is Agro Eco-System Analysis?

Glossary

Ability: An individual's capacity to perform the various tasks in a job.

Accountability: is an obligation on the part of the subordinates to perform the duties.

Active Listening: The active search for meaning when one listens.

Affiliation Need: The desire for friendly and close interpersonal relationships.

Auditing: It is the process of appraisal and it is associated with detecting fraud.

Authoritarianism: The belief that there should be status and power difference among people in organizations.

Authority: The power to make decisions, which guide actions of others.

Authority: The rights inherent in a managerial position to give orders and expect the orders to be obeyed.

Autocratic Leader: One who dictates decisions down to subordinates.

Autonomy: The degree to which the job provides substantial freedom and discretion to the individual in scheduling the work and in determining the procedures to be used in carrying it out.

Bases of Power: What power holders control that allows them to manipulate the behaviour of others.

Budget: It is a statement of expected results in numerical terms.

Budget: It is an estimate of future needs arranged according to an orderly basis, covering some or all of the activities of an enterprise for a definite period of time.

Budgetary Control: It involves the use of budgets and budgetary reports throughout the period to coordinate, evaluate and control day-to-day operations in accordance with the goal specified by the budget.

Case Study: An in-depth analysis of one setting.

Centralization: The degree to which decision making is concentrated at a single point in the organization.

Chain of Command: The superior-subordinate authority relationship that extends from the top of the organization to the lowest.

Change: Making things different.

Channel: The medium through which a communication message travels.

Committee: A group of persons formed for a special purpose.

Communication Networks: Channels by which information flows.

Communication Process: The steps between a source and a receiver that result in the transference of meaning.

Conceptual Skills: The mental abilities to analyze and diagnose complex situations.

Conflict: A process in which an effort is purposely made by A to offset the efforts of B by some form of blocking that will result in frustrating B in attaining his or her goals or furthering his or her interests.

Controlling: comparing results with the plans and taking corrective actions when the results deviate from the plans.

Coordination: It is a process by which group efforts are made in orderly sequence and unity of action is ensured in the pursuit of a common objective.

Decentralization: It refers to dispersal of decision making authority.

Decision-making: It is the selection, based on some criteria from two/ more possible alternatives.

Decision Support System: It uses computers to facilitate the decision making process of semi structured tasks.

Decisional Roles: Roles that include those of entrepreneur, disturbance handler, resource allocator and negotiator.

Delegation: It means assigning work to others and giving them authority to do it.

Departmentation: It implies the grouping of various activities on the basis of their similarity into separate units.

Division of Labour: The break down of jobs into narrow, repetitive tasks.

Effectiveness: Achievement of goal.

Efficiency: The ratio of effective output to the input required to achieve it.

Employee Oriented Leader: One who emphasizes interpersonal relations.

Equity Theory: Individuals compare their job inputs and outcomes with those of others and then respond so as to eliminate any inequities.

ERG Theory: There are three groups of core needs, existence, relatedness and growth.

Expectancy Theory: The strength of a tendency to act in a certain way depends on the strength of an expectation that the act will be followed by a given outcome and on the attractiveness of that outcome to the individual.

Expert Power: Influence based on special skills or knowledge.

Extrinsic Rewards: Rewards received from the environment surrounding the context of the work.

Grapevine: The informal communication channel.

Hierarchy of Needs Theory: There is hierarchy of five needs-physiological, safety, love, esteem and self actualization and as each need is sequentially satisfied the next need becomes dominant.

Higher Order Needs: Needs that are satisfied internally needs for love, esteem and self actualization.

HR Audit: Study of existing manpower resources of the organization.

Human Resource: Refers to the knowledge, skills, creative abilities, talents and aptitudes of an organization work force as well as the individuals involved.

Human Skills: The ability to work with, understand and motivate other people both individually and in groups.

Hygiene Factors: Those factors such as company policy and administration, supervision and salary that when present in a job place. When these factors are present people will not be dissatisfied.

Informational Roles: Roles that include monitoring, disseminating and spokesperson activities.

Intellectual Ability: The ability required to do mental activities.

Interpersonal Roles: Roles that include figure head, leadership and liaison activities.

Intrinsic Rewards: The pleasure or value one receives from the content of a work task.

Job Analysis: Developing a detailed description of the tasks involved in a job, determining the relationship of a given job to other jobs and ascertaining the knowledge, skills and abilities necessary for an employee to perform the job successfully.

Job Description: A written statement of what a job holder does, how it is done and why it is done.

Job Design: The way that tasks are combined to form complete Jobs.

Job Enlargement: The horizontal expansion of jobs.

Job-Enrichment: The vertical expansion of jobs.

Job Involvement: The degree to which a person identifies with his or her job, actively participates in it and considers his or her performance important to his or her sense of self worth.

Job Rotation: The periodic shifting of a worker from one task to other.

Job Satisfaction: A general attitude towards one's job, the difference between the amount they believe they should receive.

Job Sharing: The practice of having two or more people split a forty hour a week job.

Job Specification: States the minimum acceptable qualifications that an employee must possess to perform a given job successfully.

Laissez-Faire: Leader permits his followers to do whatever they want to do.

Leadership: The ability to influence a group towards the achievement of goals.

Leading: Includes motivating subordinates, directing others, selecting the most effective communication channels and resolving conflicts.

Line Authority: Authority that entitles a manager to direct the work of a subordinate.

Low Level Management: They are concerned with day-to-day planning and implement the policies of middle management.

Management by Objectives: A program that encompasses specific goals, participative set for an explicit time period with feedback on goal progress.

Managers: Individuals who achieves goals through other people.

Matrix or Grid Organization: It is a hybrid structure combining two complementary structures—functional departmentation with pure project structure.

MBO: It is a comprehensive managerial system that integrates many key managerial activities in a systematic manner, consciously directed towards the effective and efficient achievement of organizational objectives.

Message: What is communicated.

Middle Management: It is basically concerned with the task of implementing the policies and plans laid down by the top management.

Motivation-Hygiene Theory: Intrinsic factors are related to job satisfaction, while extrinsic factors are associated with dissatisfaction.

Motivation: The willingness to exert high levels of effort towards organizational goals, conditioned by the effort's ability to satisfy some individual needs.

Need: Some internal state that makes certain outcomes appear attractive.

Non-verbal Communication: Messages conveyed through body movements, the intonations or emphasis we give towards facial expressions and the physical distance between the sender and receiver.

Objectives: They are the end results towards which activities are aimed.

Organization: Determining the activities to accomplish a job and arrange the distribution of activities among the people.

Organizational Behaviour: A field of study that investigates the impact that individuals, groups and structure have on behaviour within organizations for the purpose of applying such knowledge towards improving an organization's effectiveness.

Organizational Commitment: An individual's orientation towards the organization in terms of loyalty, identification and involvement.

Organizational Culture: Common perception held by the organization's members, a system of shared meaning.

Organizational Development: A collection of techniques that attempt to effect systematic planned change.

Organizational Structure: The degree of complexity, formalization and centralization in the organization.

Organizing: Determining what tasks are to be done, who is to do them, how the tasks are to be grouped, who reports to whom and where decisions are to be made.

Participatory Rural Appraisal: It is a methodology for interacting with villagers, understanding them and learning from them.

PERT: It is a sophisticated, mathematical and schematic network technique used for planning and control.

Placement: The process of placing the right man on the right job.

Planned Change: Change activities that are intentional and goal oriented.

Planning: Includes defining goals, establishing strategy and developing plans to coordinate activities.

Planning: It means the determination of what is to be done, how and where it is to be done, who is to do it and how results are to be evaluated.

Policies: They are general statements/understandings, which guide thinking in a decision making, leaving it to the managers to decide within its framework.

Position Power: Influence derived from one's formal structural position in the organization, includes power to hire, fire, discipline, promote and give salary increments.

Power: A capacity that A has to influence the behaviour of B so that B does things he or she would not otherwise do.

Procedures: They are guides to action rather than to thinking and indicate the exact manner in which activities must be accomplished.

Productivity: A performance measure includes effectiveness and efficiency.

Professional Bureaucracy: A structure that rates high in complexity and formalization and low in centralization.

Programme: It is a sequence of activity to be implemented and specifies a step-by-step approach to guide the action to achieve the goal.

Project: A project is a small programme and it has a definite goal concerning task assignment and time.

Purpose/Mission: It is the basic intention of an organization based on which other actions are designed.

Referent Power: Influence held by A on B's admiration and desire to model himself or herself after A.

Responsibility: It is the obligation of a subordinate to whom a superior has assigned a task, to perform the service as required.

Role Conflict: A situation in which an individual is confronted by divergent role expectations.

Role Expectations: How others believe a person should act in a given situation.

Role Identity: Certain attitudes and behaviour consistent with a role.

Role Perception: An individual's view of how he or she is supposed to act in a given situation.

Role: A set of expected behaviour patterns attributed to someone occupying a given position in a social unit.

Rules: It prescribes in advance what is to be done or not to be done in a specific situation.

Schedule: It is a process of establishing a time sequence for the work to be done.

Scientific Management: Means knowing exactly what you want men to do and seeing that they do it in the best and the cheapest way.

Self-actualization: The drive to become what one is capable of becoming.

Self-esteem: Individual's degree of liking or disliking for themselves.

Self-management: Learning techniques that allow individuals to manage their own behaviour so that less external management control is necessary.

Self-monitoring: A personality trait that measures an individual's ability to adjust his or her behaviour to external, situational factors.

Sensitivity Trailing: Training groups that seek to change behaviour through unstructured group interaction.

Sources of Power: How power holders come to control the bases of power.

Span of Control: The number of subordinates a manager can direct efficiently and effectively.

Span of Management: refers to the optimum number of subordinates a manager can manage or control effectively.

Staff Authority: Authority that supports, assists and advises.

Strategy: It concerns with how the organization plans to meet the uncertain and competitive world outside.

SWOT: It is an acronym for Strengths, Weaknesses, Opportunities and Threats.

Technical Skills: The ability to apply specialized knowledge or expertise.

Technology: How an organization transfers its inputs into outputs.

Theory X: The assumption that employees dislike work, are lazy, dislike responsibility and must be coerced to perform.

Theory Y: The assumption that employees like work, are creative, seek responsibility and can exercise self direction.

Theory: A set of systematically interrelated concepts or hypotheses that purport to explain and predict phenomenon.

Three Needs Theory: Achievement, power and affiliation are three important needs that help to understand motivation.

Top Management: It is the ultimate source of management authority and it is accountable for overall management to the shareholders of the company.

Unity of Command: A subordinate should have only one superior to whom he or she is directly responsible.

References

Banerjee, A.K., Nair, R.K. and Agrawal, V.K. 2003. *Principles and Practice of Management*. Pragati Prakashan, Meerut, p. 293.

Borker, D. 1980. *Transactional Analysis and Training—The Theory and Use of Transactional Analysis in Organization*. Grier Press, UK, p. 255.

Chatterjee, S.S. 1988. *Introduction to Management, Its Principles and Techniques*. World Press, Calcutta, p. 345.

Dahama, O.P. and Bhatnagar, O.P. 1985. *Education and Communication for Development*. Oxford and IBH Publishing Company Pvt. Ltd., New Delhi, p. 734.

Gordon, B. and Margrette, H.O.1985. *Management Information System—Concept, Foundation and Structure*. Tata McGraw Hill Company Pvt. Ltd., New York, p. 285.

James, A.F. Stoner and Freeman, R.E. 1994. *Management*. Prentice Hall, New Delhi, p. 320.

Kumar, Birendra and Hansra, B.S. 2000. Extension *Education for Human Resource Development*. Concept Publishing Company, New Delhi, p. 200.

Pulaparampil John, 1999. *A Handbook on Total Quality Management in Government*. Institute of Management in Government, Thiruvananthapuram, p. 133.

Ray, G.L. 2003. *Extension Communication and Management*. Fifth edition. Kalyani Publishers, New Delhi, p. 382.

Reddin, W.J. 1971. *Effective Management by Objectives—The Three Method of MBO*. Tata McGraw Hill, New Delhi.

Singh, P.N. 1999. *Training for Management Development*. Suchandra Publications, New Delhi, p. 210.

Tripathi, P.C. 2003. *Human Resource Development*. Sultan Chand and Sons. Educational Publishers, New Delhi, p. 379.

Van den Ban, A.W. and Hawkins, H.S. 1998. *Agricultural Extension*. CBS Publishers, New Delhi, p. 294.

Vijayaraghavan, K. and Hansra, B.S. 2001. *A Manual on Training Management*. Indian Council of Agricultural Research, New Delhi, p. 160.